THOSE IN PERIL ON THE SEA
USS Bassett rescues 152 survivors of the USS Indianapolis

L. Peter Wren
LCDR USNR ret
Rescue boat officer at the scene

Published in Richmond, Virginia
1999

THOSE IN PERIL ON THE SEA
USS Bassett rescues 152 survivors
of the USS Indianapolis

First Printing: July 1999
Second Printing: August 1999

ISBN 0-9622084-3-4 (softcover)
ISBN 0-9622084-2 (hardcover)

Library of Congress Catalog Card Number
99-93999

A portion of the sales price of this book will be
donated to create an educational fund for the grandchildren of
the Indianapolis crew, the Bassett crew and Naval Sea Cadets
of the Richmond Council of the United States Navy League.

Book cover by William W. McCathern, Jr
Published in Richmond, Virginia.

Dedication

This book is dedicated to the men of the USS Bassett who gave of themselves and of their possessions to bring reality back to the Indy survivors from the fear driven, death laden, hallucinations of the sea, the sharks and the sun. One had to be at the rescue scene to know of the acts of bravery, and compassion freely and tenderly given by these men.

These sacrifices and many more happened at the scene. Crew members jumped from their boats into the turbulent sea, to cut survivors loose from the floating nets, survivors who tied themselves to the nets so that they would not drift away from the group. Rescuers had to calm the survivor who thought he was being attacked by a "Jap" coming to capture him. Crew members stayed in the sea boosting survivors too weak to climb into the boats. They cut away the life jacket that was slowly drowning the semi-comatose survivor. All these acts and many more happened in a darken and angry midnight sea.

The ship crew members carefully and tenderly lifted survivors covered with bunker oil, salt water ulcers, and small fish bites aboard ship. Crew members cut off clothing so oil ladened that it couldn't be unbuttoned; and they applied diesel oil carefully to clean survivors and then washed them with soap. They listened to their screams when the diesel oil burned in the open wounds, the ulcers, and the chafed areas around the neck and arms caused by the life jackets. Medical personnel moved from man to man giving individual instructions best for each survivor.

Bassett sailors assisted those who had to vomit the oil and sea water they had ingested after five days in the ocean. Crew members brought personal clothing from their lockers and helped dress the Indianapolis victims. Cooks never closed the food line and catered to every request within their power to prepare.

There are no greater shipmates than those men from the USS Bassett. Their recognition and thank you is long over due.

USS BASSETT APD - 73

Acknowledgements

This book is the product of the men who were either survivors, rescuers or others who aided in the rescue when the USS Indianapolis was sunk by a Japanese submarine July 30, 1945 in the Philippine Sea.

Fortunately, I am able to relate the stories of many of the men who suffered through this tragedy as well as those who helped in the rescue of them. Recognition is also given to the many who helped the author create this volume, because their words tell what it was like and they, like the author, are still marked by this tragedy.

Encouragement and direct help came especially from my shipmates Jack Paul, Ray and Earle Houghtaling. Computer help was graciously given by Henry Scott, Martin Finnerty, Jackie Willey, Donna B. Gilliam, Lynn Palmer and Linda Held Wren. My special thanks to my wife Helen M. Wren who freed me of duties so I could continue to get the written material on the computer.

Crossing the "Ts" and dotting the "Is" belongs to my consulting editor Charles F. Finley, Jr. My Navy League associate, William W. McCathern, created the art work which has enhanced the various stories. My gratitude is extended to both of them.

Lastly my thanks goes to my Navy League friends of the Richmond Virginia Council who encouraged me to create this volume, lest the story be lost as many sailors of the World War 11 generation are making the "roll call" topside!

An overview of the contents of this book

Chapter One

Introduces the title of the book and the USS Bassett and the USS Indianapolis. William Ault's words set the scene of the tragedy. The few "sea stories" given illustrates the spirit of the Bassett and are similar to what crews from any ship would tell.

Chapter Two

Oral histories as told by the Bassett Crew rescuing the survivors from the ocean.

Chapter Three

Pictures and Drawings by
William W. McCathern, Jr.

Chapter Four

Oral histories of the USS Indianapolis Survivors describing the sinking and the rescue.

Chapter Five

Oral histories and stories of others who are related to the survivors, or who were part of the medical teams caring for the survivors, or were the airplane crew plus a list of the Bassett crew.

Chapter One

Introduces the title of this book and the oral histories of the rescue of the USS Indianapolis survivors by the USS Bassett and other ships at the rescue scene.

An overview by William F. Ault details the fears and suffering of the survivors. Also are several short "Sea Stories" told by Bassett crew members.

Those in Peril on the Sea
USS Bassett rescues 152 survivors
of the USS Indianapolis
by
L. Peter Wren
A Boat Officer from the USS Bassett [APD73]*

The title of this book is inspired by the last line in the US Navy Hymn which describes well the situation the USS Indianapolis' crew found themselves in after having delivered the atomic bomb parts to the Island of Tinian. The crew knew they were on a secret mission but had no idea of the importance of their mission. At twelve minutes after midnight on the 30th of July 1945 the USS Indianapolis with a crew of 1197 on board was sunk in the Philippine Sea. Approximately 880 of the 1197 crew were able to abandon ship. Some made it with life jackets while others just dove into the sea hoping to find some floating debris to cling to until help came. Life nets and life jackets were cut free by some crew members before they left the ship. Those with life jackets supported others until life rafts and floating nets broke free from the sinking ship. Five nights passed before ships were directed to the survivors' area. The mission was top secret and confusion between commands of different areas of the Pacific resulted in a gap in the communications. The USS Bassett, while patrolling off the Island of Leyte of the Philippine Islands, received an urgent message to "proceed to a given latitude and longitude and to investigate unknown objects in the water". The Bassett recovered 152 men of the 317 that were rescued.

The shipmates of the Bassett have prevailed upon the author to produce this book because of his actual experience that night believing that he could best tell the

---

* Definition of Naval Abbreviations given on page 192.

story. However the author has attempted to coordinate the oral histories of both the survivors and the rescue crew as the best way to tell the story.

An American patrol airplane while trying to repair special aerial looked down on the Philippine Sea and discovered a group of floating men. The patrol had no previous information on any sinkings in the Philippine Sea so they opened up on their radio circuit to alert military commands and thereby set the rescue mission into motion. Truly this was a great tragedy. As you read these oral histories you will learn of man's compassion for his fellow man. Those of us who were part of this have been deeply touched and marked for the rest of our lives. We shall never forget that dark night, that sea, the sharks and the plight of the survivors. We were in most cases just young men called on to be our brother's keeper. Though more than fifty years have passed since the sinking, we here again recite the first verse of our Navy Hymn for your prayerful reading, which is the source of the book's title.

THE NAVY HYMN

Eternal Father strong to save
Whose arm does rule the restless wave
Who biddest the mighty ocean deep
Its own appointed limits keep
Oh hear us when we pray to thee
For those in peril on the sea.

Dear Mr Wren:

July 30, 1945, the day of the sinking had been a very nice day. A group of us from the radar division had been playing cards all afternoon. When one or two of us would drop out to go on watch, someone else would take his place in the game. When chow time came around in the evening, we didn't bother eating because not too many of our fellows cared for the cold cuts we always had on Sunday evenings.

My watch station at this time was on the fire control radar on the 40MM guns. This station was located below the 40MM guns that were just aft the signal bridge. I had just gone on watch at 11:45 pm Sunday night July 30, had checked my radar set and had checked in with the gun crew to make sure everything was okay. When the guns weren't being used we kept the fire control radar on a standby condition. During this time I had nothing to do but to keep in contact with the gun crew by telephone. It was very close to midnight when the torpedoes hit. No one knew the explosion was a torpedo. With the explosion, the lights dimmed and went out. The other man that was in the fire control room and I stepped out of our compartment to see what was going on. I heard one person, I don't know who it was, say, "Hurrah, one of the boilers just blew up and it is back to the states for us!" I don't know whether he survived or not.

When we stepped out of our compartment to the port side, the ship was already beginning to list to the starboard. There were quite a few men standing on deck waiting for some word to be passed over the loud speaker as to what had happened and whether they should go to their battle stations, or abandon ship stations. The word was never passed because the power had been knocked out when the torpedoes hit.

When no word was passed, an officer standing with us told a couple of sailors to break out the life preservers. We all put them on and about this time the ship was in a 45 to a 60 degree list to starboard.

The officer told us that we had better leave the ship, so a couple of lines were thrown over the port side and we could almost walk down the side of the ship at this time. I grabbed the line and went over the side walking and slipping until I was close enough to the water to jump. As soon as I hit the water I started swimming as hard as I could to get away from the sinking ship that could pull you under. I swam about 50 to 100 yards from the ship and then glanced around to see what was happening. Right then the only part of the ship was the fantail with four screws sticking out of the water. I started swimming again to get away as far as possible, and the next time I looked the ship was gone. At that time, as far as I knew, I was the only one left. No one else was near me that I could see, and I had been too busy up until now to listen. This happened in 15 minutes or less and there was no time to think of anything but survival. I heard voices a short time later and I swam around until I spied a few men clinging together. Some were sick from swallowing salt water, but our biggest concern at this time was that we were afraid if we had been sunk by a submarine, it would surface and open fire on us in the water.

Many things went through my head as I was going over the side of the ship into the water. I thought my time had come and I was wondering what my wife and son would do. After the initial shock of the sinking had worn off, we were beginning to group up in the water. I had made up my mind at that time that if I did lose my life in the water I would be one of the last ones to go. I think this determination was what kept me from losing my sanity, which is what many of my shipmates did.

When I went over the side I was wearing a blue denim shirt, dungarees and shoes and socks. Some of the men had on only shorts and no shirts, some even had less. I had no injuries and I didn't get sick from swallowing sea water. Some of the men weren't as lucky. During the sinking a few life rafts had floated away from the ship and each one had two or three men in them. In the group I was in, we tied the rafts together and the men who couldn't get in the rafts hung on to the sides. I don't remember when we found the floater net, whether it was the first night or after daylight of the first day, but it was a real lifesaver. We tied three or four of the rafts to the floater net and by doing this we had a place to hang on to which was not as tiresome as hanging on to the rafts. Also, during the first night, we kept picking up more men and we were running out of space for them to hang on the sides of the rafts. I didn't think we would be picked up that night but I was sure when daylight came help would be there. We all thought that an SOS [save our ship] had been sent out and help would come quickly.

That first night seemed like it would never come to an end. Finally daybreak came and everyone began looking for our rescue ship. We saw planes fly overhead and tried to signal them but they never knew we were there. As the day progressed we began to wonder if we would be rescued by nightfall. Our spirits were very low. During the first day we checked to see what supplies we had aboard the rafts. We had three casks of water, and a few malted milk tablets. The water, we found out later in the day, was brackish and we could not drink it. We also found a signal flare gun with a few flares.

During the day, the sharks would come around and when anyone shouted "sharks!" everyone would splash the water, kick their feet and make noise to try to drive them away. As long as we floated in the oil slick, which would come and go, the sharks wouldn't bother us. I guess the sharks were afraid of the darkness, and the shadow of the oil kept them away. The nights on the water were better than the days in some ways because at night we didn't worry about the sharks and we didn't have the sun beating down on us. Our kapoks [life jackets] were beginning to get soaked and we kept sinking lower in the water every day. A kapok was supposed to be good for 48 to 72 hours.

The second night out I was hanging onto the floated net and dozed off for a short time. When I woke up there was no one around me. I had let go of the net while I dozed and had floated away from the group. I didn't know which way to swim to rejoin them and I was trying to decide what to do when I heard their voices. It didn't take me long to rejoin them and from that time on, I kept myself tied to the net.

I think my only other narrow escape from death came on the last day we were in the water. Many of the men at that time were becoming delirious and were seeing drinking fountains, soda fountains, or coffee urns under the water. Or they thought they saw the ship's messhall where the drinking fountain and the "Joe" pots of coffee were. On this day one of the men told me he was going below to get a drink and wanted me to go with him. I agreed and he went under the water to go below. I started to follow but when the water went over my head I had enough presence of mind left to realize that there was nothing there but water.

I don't remember much about the rescue except that when the Bassett crew on the LCVP pulled me aboard I thought my arms would give out before I got aboard. I don't know if I walked on to the ship or if I was carried to a lower bunk. While I was lying or sleeping there, I was awakened by the man above me who was urinating and it was seeping through the upper canvas bunk on to me. I looked up and saw a crewman nearby. He saw that I was awake and asked me if I would like him to try to clean me up. I agreed. He took me into the shower and washed me first with diesel fuel.

7

One wash wasn't enough so he was washing me again when he said: " My God, I have a blonde!"

I can't thank your Bassett shipmates enough for their gentle and loving care. I didn't know that men could be so kind and thoughtful.

/s/Wm. F. Ault, Sr

Note from the author. As a shipboard routine the water casks and rations in the whale boats and LCVPs were inspected every two weeks. The water in the casks was always replaced at this time and the "C" rations and malted milk tablets were also counted and replaced if necessary. It seems that the crew members who liked a little snack at night would sneak a few of the malted milk tablets out of the ration boxes. We never found out who was taking them, and a warning as to how important they were to the life boats {LCVPs} never seemed to stop the culprits. I was not surprised when Wm. Ault said there were only a few malt tablets on the life raft. As to the brackish water found in the water casks, I surmise the seaman who had the duty to fill them mistakenly got his water from a fire main rather than getting the water from the ships galley {think kitchen}.

The USS Indianapolis [CA35]

Source: Ships History, US Naval Institute, Annapolis, MD

The USS Indianapolis' keel was laid on 31 March 1930 by the New York Shipbuilding Corporation, Camden N.J. Launching took place on 7 November 1931 and was sponsored by Miss Lucy Taggart, daughter of then Senator Thomas Taggart. The ship was commissioned in the Philadelphia Navy Yard on 15 November 1932 and was sunk by a Japanese submarine in the Philippine Sea on 30 July 1945 in its thirteenth year of operation in defense of the United States. The final mission of the USS Indianapolis was to deliver the atomic bomb parts to Tinian Island in the Marianas for its eventual air drop on Hiroshima, Japan. The tragic loss of this ship and 880 crew members will always be remembered, for this is the ship whose "historic run" introduced the atomic weapon into warfare. Never again would the world be the same.

From the beginning the Indianapolis was labeled as a special ship of the Portland Class of Cruisers. Franklin D. Roosevelt {FDR} was Assistant Secretary of the Navy in 1913 under President Woodrow Wilson. The Officer's Country aboard the USS Indianapolis had an elevator installed to accommodate FDR and a fully equipped mahogany bar. It was given the gracious title "The Pride of the Fleet!" Prior to WWII the ship had so many state and foreign visitors that the crew often joked, we were worried that the ship might sink due to all the--Brass--we carry around.

This Cruiser had a length of 610 feet, a width of 66 feet, and a draft of 17'4" which allowed the Indy to bring her guns' firepower closer to shore. The Indy's speed was stated at 32 knots and she carried nine 8" guns and eight 5" guns. The crew was originally set at 1269 men. On the fatal voyage

9

the Indy carried only 1197 men. Due to the Washington Treaty of 1929 following the end of WW I heavy cruisers then being built had to adhere to strict guidelines to which all seapower nations had agreed. Under the Treaty, cruisers, so as not to be categorized as "warships," were limited to 10,000 tons gross weight. The Indianapolis' displacement was 9800 tons. To come under this weight, and meet Treaty requirements, the normal "blisters" which are extra heavy armor plates would not be attached to the Indianapolis hull. This armor plating ran on both sides of the ship from bow to stern. The armor plate or "blister" protected "warships" from torpedoes and mines. When a "warship" is hit by a torpedo or a mine the damage is usually to the blister and not to the hull of the ship. By damage control measures and counter flooding the "warship" is returned to a level gun platform and continues the battle. By not having the "blister" plating the Indy was vulnerable to easy hull damage. To the ship's advantage by not having the "blisters" she had greater speed and less draft permitting entry into shallow coastal waters. This last feature meant she could rake the beach with gun fire before the landing parties went ashore. The Indy continued to be the Flagship for the remainder of her peacetime career and welcomed FDR at Charlestown S.C. on 18 November 1936 for the "Good Neighbor Cruise" to South America. After transporting FDR to Rio de Janerio, Buenos Aires and Montivedo for state visits the Indy returned to Charleston, SC on 15 December 1936 where the President and party departed the ship. It was on the USS Indy that FDR was awarded his "shellback" status in the Kingdom of Neptune Rex for having crossed the Equator. It is recorded that FDR was given a pair of fire nozzles to watch for Davey Jones and was ordered to fish with a bent pin in a large steel pot. Davey Jones is a personality of the sea. Any American sailor crossing the equator for the first time is entering into Davey Jones' realm and a proper initiation is conducted aboard the ship to change the sailor's status from a lowly pollywog to a shellback. A shellback has faced the full rigors of the sea and is a worthy member of Davey Jones' realm. A pollywog by trial and initiation must prove his worthiness to become a full member. A senior enlisted man is elected to conduct the ceremony and all officers, guests and enlisted who have never crossed the equator must submit to the trial. Usually it is a fun packed event for all hands aboard.

When the Japanese struck Pearl Harbor on 7 December 1941 the Indy was making simulated bombardment exercises 300 miles away on Johnson Island, and immediately joined Task Force 12 searching for Japanese carriers reported to be still in the Pearl Harbor vicinity. Upon the return to Pearl Harbor in December she continued to search for the enemy with her scouting airplanes since "radar gear" had not been available at the time.

On 10 March 1942 in conjunction with the carrier USS Lexington, the USS Indy carried the war to the Japanese 350 miles south of Rabaul to the Island of New Britain. Her next engagement was with Task Force 12 where she reinforced the US carrier USS Yorktown in the enemy port of Lae and Salamaua of New Guinea. In the 36 months that followed the USS Indy was involved with the enemy as follows:

> Kiska and the Aleutian Islands
> Tarawa and Kwajalein
> Palau
> Peleliu
> Bonine and Volcanic Islands
> Marianas with Tinian and Saipan
> The Battle of the Philippine Sea
> (a.k.a the Turkey Shoot)
> First ship to re-enter Apra Harbor on Guam
> The Tokyo Raid on the Home Islands
> The Battle at Iwo Jima

11

The Battle at Okinawa.
{31 March 1945}

On 31 March 1945 just two days before the invasion of Okinawa a single Japanese plane broke out of the morning mist and in spite of twenty millimeter fire the kamakasi was able to crash his plane on the port aft portion of the ship and splash over the side. The bomb he carried was dropped about 25 feet above the fantail, passed completely through the armor deck and out the bottom of the Indy. The bomb exploded in the water below the ship and the concussion blew two gaping holes in the ship's bottom, flooding compartments in the area. Nine of the ship's crew were killed and the ship settled slightly to the stern with a port list. The injured vessel made its way to a salvage ship for emergency repairs. With a devoted crew, the Indy made the long voyage to Mare Island Navy Yard in California for repairs.

Continuing with the history of the Indy, the repairs were completed and a special mission is now brewing. On 16 July 1945 many of the crew and officers were issued recalls from their well earned "leaves"; some never did get to call home or say a fond farewell to loved ones. The ship left San Francisco with orders to get this special crate (Black Box) welded to the deck, to Tinian Island in the Marianas as quickly as possible. President Harry Truman's message to Commanding officer Captain McVay read to the effect: "Don't let anything happen to this crate. If you must, put it in a whale boat to save it, above all, save it. This mission could shorten the war by days! "

The transit across the Pacific, with a two hour refueling stop at Pearl Harbor on the 19th took ten days and set a new record. Relieved of the cargo on 26 July at Tinian Island with still no knowledge what the "Black Box" contained, the Indy now proceeded to the southern most island in the chain known as Guam. Here the Indy was refueled and replenished. On the 28 July 1945 the Indy departed Guam heading across the Philippine Sea. The old timers aboard recited to new crew members, the vivid details of the "Great Turkey Shoot" that had occurred on these waters several months earlier.

The ship has been buttoned up tight since it left San Francisco because of the "Black Box" aboard. Knowing that another operation will begin when they reach Leyte Island, it might be well to let the crew relax a little in this crossing to the Philippines. According to the latest intelligence reports from Guam there are no known enemy craft on the path the Indy will travel. Since it has such great speed, it can out run and out gun most any vessel the enemy may have out there. No escort vessel was provided. If the reader has never been on a man-o-war in the South Pacific he doesn't understand that the hot sun bakes the thick armor deck all day and then radiates that heat all night. Sleeping below is very hot, sweaty and odoriferous. Fresh cool air is hard to come by when you are below the main deck. Shipmates adjust to this--but if the Captain will let you sleep out on the deck at night--wow what a relief! Many mates find a spot to sack out on the open deck. Their mattress pad insulates them from the hot deck and shoes become a pillow. Small talk with the mate next to him doesn't last long as the ship's speed creates a fresh breeze. The 28th and 29th of July are the usual ship-board routines and a chance to get to know some of the new mates. The usual tricks are played on the new green shipmates who are sent seeking 50 feet of shore line for the Boatswain Mate or a bucket of steam from the ship's galley to repair a blivit.

It was on the 30th of July at midnight when the Japanese torpedoes punctured the Indy's hull. Remember, the "blisters" were never installed and now the Achilles heel has been found; the USS Indianapolis sunk in 12 minutes. The Indy's devoted crew found the ship in peril in the thirteenth year of its defense of the United States of America. A ship that fought from below the equator in the South Pacific to the

13

shores of Japan now will miss the victory it so arduously help win. The ship which helped introduce atomic warfare to the world, will take with it two-thirds of its crew.

The history does not end here, for the survivors go on to tell again the acts of brotherly love that followed in the Philippine Sea. The rescue crews who labored on the fifth night after the sinking are marked by this tragedy. There are sights and sounds ever fresh in their ears and eyes as they went about lifting these near dead men from the sea. The following is one such story from the USS Bassett which rescued 152 of the 317 survivors. The oral histories are from my shipmates on the Bassett as well as from survivors who were rescued that night by the USS Bassett and other ships which arrived soon after. Later we learned of the communication errors that occurred in war weary dedicated men who failed to follow up on events that normally would be handled with military precision. A single message was sent to the USS Idaho indicating that the USS Indianapolis was enroute from Guam and would replace the Idaho as the "Flag Ship" of the 5th fleet.

The U.S. Navy operators in Guam received a confirmation that the USS Indy was to occupy a certain anchorage area in the Leyte Harbor. The Estimated Time of Arrival (ETA) was known, but when the Indy did not show up, a note was made on the arrival board that the Indy was still expected. Since there was no new ETA, and since CINCPAC (Commander in Chief Pacific Fleet) had directed not to report "Major War" vessels movements, the information was posted on the communication board awaiting a followup report. The USS Idaho said the message received was garbled but never asked for a repeat of the message. The Philippine Sea at that time in the war was known as the "back water" of the Navy's war in the Pacific. Captain McVay was never informed of the enemy submarines present and he was dispatched from Guam to Leyte without benefit of any

14

destroyer escort. Since the Indy had traveled alone before, it didn't seem unusual for her to be ordered to travel the open sea alone again. It was generally felt that the Imperial Navy of Japan was of no threat in that area.

The survivors' rescue began when a pilot on an American airplane, on patrol, while adjusting his aerial, saw an oil slick on the surface of the Philippine Sea and flew down to search for an enemy submarine. Herewith are the oral histories of the survivors, rescuers, medics and others who had these men in their care after their five day ordeal with the sun, the sea and the sharks. These oral histories, I believe tell this story best. I thank those who have helped me record it for generations to come.

The USS Indianapolis had earned ten Battle Stars, made the "Historic Run," carried the atomic bomb, which did in fact shorten the war. The USS Indianapolis deserves a special place in American Naval history. In addition to the 880 men who were lost with the sinking of the Indy, one of the saddest losses of this ship was the loss of number 881, the Captain Charles B. McVay, III. He was court martialed by his peers for failing to "zig zag" the course of the ship and failure to give the command "abandon ship." The oral histories given herein will permit the readers to draw their own conclusions.

HEAVY CRUISER USS INDIANAPOLIS CA-35
Sank July 30, 1945 in 12 minutes, after taking two torpedo hits
from the Japanese submarine I-58

15

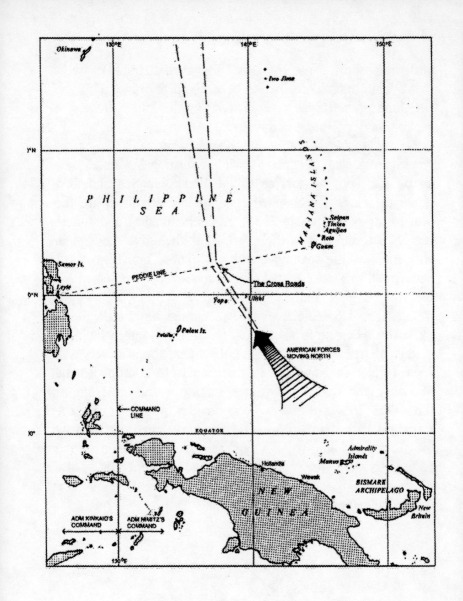

The Rescue Message

The location of the "Command Line" is important in that its location tends to explain some of the communication problems which affected the survivors of the Indianapolis. Also by having an understanding of its location, operations in the area around the Philippine Sea Frontier [PSF] are a little clearer. This line also helps explain the USS Bassett's assignments in this area.

The war was proceeding rapidly north with the recapture of the Philippine Islands on October 20, 1944 by General MacArthur's Troops and with the strong assistance of US Naval Forces. Headquarters for the Philippine Sea Frontier were set up by Admiral Kauffman in Tolosa which is just twenty miles south of the large city of Tacloban on Leyte Island. Adm. Kauffman's command encompassed the large area west of 130 degrees east longitude from Malayasia and Borneo south to about 20 degrees north latitude which is just above Luzon Island of the Philippines.

Admiral Thomas C. Kinkaid wore two hats in those days. He commanded the 7th fleet based in Manila and the Allied Naval Forces of the Southwest Pacific which included the Philippine Sea Frontier {PSF}. Often the Allied Naval Forces of the Southwest Pacific were referred to as "MacArthur's Navy." Operations from Guam including the sea area east of the 130 degree longitude was commanded by Admiral Chester Nimitz. The "Command Line" at 130 degrees east longitude separated the commands of Nimitz and the Kinkaid.

The USS Bassett was part of the PSF and was called on to escort vessels to Hollandia, New Guinea and served as "fast" transport throughout the Philippine Islands, and the south China Sea. On July 21, 1945 the Bassett operating with the PSF enroute from Leyte carried troops to: Cebu City on

17

Cebu Island; Zamboanga on Mindanao Island; Brunei Bay on Borneo; Puerto Princessa on Palawan Island; Iloilo on Panay Island; to Macajalar Bay and then returned to Leyte Island for further assignment.

We were then replenished and refueled and enjoyed an "R & R" stop (rest & recreation) at the Tacloban Naval Facility. It was then that we picked up the "oranges" that you will read about later. On 31 July 1945 we were enroute from Leyte to Station D near the "Peddie" line. The "Peddie" line was the sea route from Guam in the Marianas to Leyte in the Philippines. At that time many Navy sea routes where given "prep school" names which could be found in the fleet operations manuals.

The intersection of the "Command Line" with the "Peddie Line" made a wide crossroads in the Philippine Sea which Japanese submarines were aware of and hung around to see what they could pick off. By the same token we knew where they were hanging around and always had a ship with proper sonar gear and depth charges probing the area. The crossroads area is where the Japanese Submarine 1-58, coming south from Japan, was operating when it discovered the USS Indianapolis making its way to Leyte unescorted.

Later I learned that the 1-58 had a special rubberized hull which requires a few statements to explain its importance. The rubberized hull would send back a mushy sonar echo to the destroyer pinging (echo ranging) on it. This mushy sound was often the echo we would receive from pinging on a whale or a group of fish. The echo from a submarine is usually a nice metallic ping. The mushy sound would cause a sonar operator to declare the echo as a false echo and cease tracking it. However depending on what you are pinging on, a propeller or the tower of a submarine, you would get a variety of echoes back plus a mushy one. A good sonar officer would search further before abandoning the echoes. Once we determined it was an enemy submarine we would roll one depth charge to drive him down and then plan our attack getting a reading on his speed, course and running depth. The above should give an overview on sonar echoing.

The Bassett departed Leyte on 31 July 1945 and continued on its next patrol mission assignment to Station D in the Philippine Sea. Our location was about 10 degrees North latitude and about 127 degrees East longitude. When on station we operate under a special task force plan for the area. On 2 August at 1240 hours we passed and exchanged calls with the USS Ringness [APD100] which was enroute to Peliliu. We continued our track in Station D--as we say in the log--"Steaming as before." At approximately 1450 hours we received an urgent message from ComPhilSeaFtr [PSF] to proceed with all speed to 11 degrees 34 minutes north and 133 degrees 47 minutes East longitude to search for survivors. The message was released 2 August at 0502 hours and we received it about nine hours later. We changed course to 066 degrees East by north east and went to flank speed. We had no idea who or what was in the water. We had a brief meeting with the Bassett LCVP crews and they were advised the survivors could be Japanese and to use caution in rescuing them. It would not be unusual for the Japanese to put a small group of men in the water as survivors to attract an American ship into their torpedo range. By our last navigational position we should be there about 1240 am. (Navy time 0040). Three boats would be waterborne and one would stay on board for last minute shipboard emergencies.

Our present location being west of the 130 degree east longitude line could have been the reason we were not aware that the destroyer escort USS Underhill, had been recently sunk by a Japanese torpedo. Since we were not operational under the Nimitz command the news of the Underhill sinking would not be directed to us. Traffic on the radio waves was very heavy and the Bassett had a low priority as an addressee for such information.

USS Bassett APD 73
From commissioning to de-commissioning

Source: Ships history, USNaval Institute, Annapolis, MD.

The USS Bassett was named in honor of Edgar R. Bassett USNR who entered the US Navy on 13 February 1940 and was subsequently commissioned Ensign, Naval Aviator USNR. Ensign Bassett participated in the battle of Midway and was killed in action on 4 June 1942. The Naval aviators in this battle, against great odds, defeated the Japanese forces and caused the loss of four Japanese carriers. The United States lost one carrier, the USS Yorktown. This battle alone set back the Japanese plans for the mid-Pacific Area and helped the American Naval forces recover from the attack on Pearl Harbor. Although Ensign Bassett's Naval service was of short duration his contribution aided in the victory of our US Naval Forces. We are proud to have served on this naval vessel honoring his name.

The concept of the naval vessel carrying the APD designation is unique. The initials stand for Attack-Passenger Destroyer and this vessel may serve as {1} an escort as do Destroyers in convoying larger ships of war; {2} as an antisubmarine vessel; {3} as a fast troop transport carrying up to 175 men and officers; {4} as an amphibious attack vessel discharging troops and/or vehicles on a beach landing, {5} as a pre-invasion force landing and recovering Underwater Demolition Teams {UDT} or Sea, Air and Land teams {SEALS} and {6} as a Harbor Entrance Control Post {HECP} in mined harbors providing charts and navigational information to ships that must enter that harbor. Because of the four LCVPs [landing craft boats which can carry vehicles or personnel] the ship has many uses and requires a crew which is readily adaptable to various needs and demands.

The Bassett was designed with a destroyer escort hull but converted to the APD concept because of the changes in the war as the American troops moved toward the Japanese home islands.

The ship had the following characteristics: Displacement- 1370 tons, length- 306 ft, beam- 37 ft, draft- 12 ft 7 inches, speed- 23 knots, complement- 204 men, guns- one 5 inch 38" caliber plus 40mm & 20mm guns, and with port and starboard Crosley engines. The Bassett was launched on 15 January 1944 as DE 672 by the Consolidated Steel Corporation Ltd. in Orange, Texas and was sponsored by Mrs Margaret Bassett, mother of Ensign Bassett. The Bassett was reclassified APD 73 on 27 June 1944. After conversion to a high-speed transport; she was commissioned on 23 February 1945. LCDR Harold J. Theriault USNR was placed in command.

The Bassett reported to the Pacific Fleet on 1 May 1945, later reported to the Commander Philippine Sea Frontier 17 July 1945, and the ship was assigned to transport passengers and mail to various Philippine Islands and Brunei Bay, Borneo. On August 2, 1945, while on anti-submarine patrol off the north coast of Leyte, the Bassett received orders to investigate reports of a large group of survivors 200 miles away. The Bassett steamed to the scene and rescued 152 of the 317 survivors from USS Indianapolis which had been sunk by a Japanese submarine at midnight on 30 July 1945. The Bassett was the second ship to arrive on the scene at midnight 3 August 1945. The total loss of men was 880 of a crew of 1197.

With the cessation of hostilities the Bassett took part in the occupation of Japan. After landing troops at Wakayama and Nagoya, the Bassett served as a harbor entrance control vessel at Nagoya until detached on 18 November 1945 and ordered to the United States carrying a full load of Naval Officers to be discharged in Pearl Harbor.

Upon arriving in San Diego, the Bassett had a short stay and then was routed on to Philadelphia via the Panama Canal. After undergoing yard availability in Philadelphia Navy Yard, the Bassett reported to Green Cove Springs, Florida for deactivation. The Bassett went out of commission and into reserve 29 April 1946.

On 7 December 1950 the Bassett was again commissioned and reported to Amphibious Forces, Atlantic Fleet where she operated between the eastern seaboard and the Caribbean Sea. Between June and August of 1952 the ship participated in a midshipman cruise to the British Isles and France. During October 1955 the Bassett was ordered to Tampico, Mexico where raging floods caused by hurricane "Janet" had engulfed 32,000 square miles of Mexican territory. While at Tampico, and working in conjunction with the USS Saipan [CVL-48] the Bassett rendered invaluable services to the distressed people by carrying supplies and rescuing those marooned by the swollen Panuco River. Between March and October 1956 she served as a unit of the amphibious task force in the Mediterranean Sea. During this cruise she took part, as primary control ship, in four amphibious operations. Reaching Little Creek, Virginia on 18 October 1956 she spent the remainder of the year in upkeep and post deployment repairs. The Bassett reported to Norfolk for inactivation and final berthing on 26 August 1957. The Bassett was decommissioned and placed in reserve on 26 November 1957. She remained inactive at Norfolk for over a decade. She was struck from the Naval Vessel Registration on 1 May 1967. She was selected for transfer to the government of Columbia and was moved to the New York Navy Yard and then to the Boston Navy Yard. After her reactivation overhaul was accomplished in early July 1968, the ship was turned over to the Columbian Navy under the Military Assistance Program. The Bassett was renamed

"Almirante Tona, DT-041, and commissioned in the Columbian Service at Boston, Mass on 6 September 1968.

This book deals with the tragedy of the loss of the Indy and the efforts of the Bassett's crew to save the survivors. But like all ships of the US Navy the crew's escapades and mishaps help to illustrate the type of men aboard and their spirit. Most assuredly the USS Indy has these tales to tell and it is the ingredient that causes the bonding among shipmates. The author includes a few stories so that one can know the Bassett crew better. In most cases the material is incongruent with the purpose of this book, but my shipmates asked me to include them.   L. Peter Wren

Breaking the Codes

Reflections by Ensign Norman DeLisle
Officer USS Bassett   Winter 1998

Ensign DeLisle in the Ship's Communications Department writes that while in Orange, Texas at the end of the day, several of the crew shipmates would get up a game of "touch football." On the last evening before they sailed for Gitmo Bay, Norman ripped the back seam out of his pants from stem to stern. Early the next morning he was hurriedly sent to the Port Communication Center to pick up the latest "Code Information" as well as the newest releases by the Communications Center so that the Bassett would be up to "speed" when they left harbor.

Upon arriving at the Port Communication Center, DeLisle was unaware he was wearing his "open air trousers." He found the offices full of very pleasant and pretty girls. The ever present smiles on the young ladies faces made him feel very welcomed, and he radiated back to them and offered verbal pleasantries. It wasn't until he got outside the office building that he felt a definite draft on his backside and then realized what he was or was not wearing. This was apparently the source of the many smiles and he definitely knew what the young lady had meant when she said: "I'll bet you were drafted into the Navy!" He had answered: "No, I was a volunteer!" Shipmates will attest that he has deciphered or broken many codes but he has never broken the "Uniform Code" again.

On another subject DeLisle commented favorably on the Supply Department's Storekeepers and Supply Officer Russell Lindsey. For morale purposes we carried several cases of 3.2 beer. Since we could be suddenly called on to transport troops to some island or atoll, storage in the Supply Departments areas was always tight and critical. There were especially heavy demands on the refrigeration space. However between Lindsey and his crew of storekeepers they had the uncanny ability to stow a monthly ration of the golden mellow liquid. They always seem to be able to replace supplies which had been consumed on the last recreation party. Such good performance was due to Ltjg Russell Lindsey's prowess as a supply officer, and it made those flat sand bar atolls a bit of South Pacific paradise.

Note: An atoll is a string of shallow coral reefs that enclose a small lagoon where ships may anchor. The larger of the islands in the atoll group are often inhabited by south pacific natives. The islands provide a source of fresh water and tropical fruit which is always welcomed by the ship's crew. During WWII the Navy took over some of the larger atolls to make recreational areas for ships crews and sometimes ship repair facilities.

/s/ N. DeLisle

Salvo on Gitmo,
April 1945

We were ordered to Guantanamo Bay on the south side of Cuba's Island where our Carribbean Naval Base is located for more fleet training prior to going to the South Pacific. We were south and east of the Harbor at Gitmo and making a simulated run on the beach as if to put a small Marine invasion group ashore. There were no Marine troops aboard and we were just running through the battle plan to be sure we would be ready when the day came to make such a run. We had gone to General Quarters and all stations reported battle ready. The ship's course was perpendicular to the beach and we were at standard speed 15 knots. LT Evans was the Officer of the Deck (OOD) and he had the junior officer of the deck (JOOD) and a quartermaster calling and plotting the bearings as we moved toward the coast of Cuba.

We were about a mile off shore and about one quarter mile from the mouth of Gitmo Bay. When we came to the line of Demarcation we would make a ninety degree turn to the right and bring our port guns to bear on the beach where the Marines were to land. The line of Demarcation is that point where the LCVP coxswain can see the beach clearly and no longer needs the ship to guide on. Being parallel to the beach where the landing will take place we bring all that ship's port guns to bear, i.e. the 20 mm, the 40 mm and the 5-inch gun. This firepower gives coverage for the landing craft to put our forces ashore.

At this moment everything is going well and to make things realistic for the crew the OOD orders Gun 51 to train to 90 degrees to left toward the beach. That was executed perfectly. So the OOD follows with the next command --Elevate to 45 degrees. And that too is carried out in a fine military manner. Then in proper sequence he orders Gun 51 to STAND BY --- Gun 51 LOAD--Gun 51 FIRE. Gun 51 responds as so ordered and the flying bridge is filled with smoke and debris from the gun muzzle. Meanwhile a shell is being hurled at Gitmo Bay. Fire control calls out "Splash!" which means watch for the splash and be prepared to call corrections, such as up 5 and right 2. The spotter, looking at the fire control chart now in use, will call the corrections. Adjustments are made to hit the target with the next salvo. Everything is going fine except the OOD should have said "THIS IS A DRILL" before he gave the command to "Train to 90 degrees to port". Quickly the OOD catches himself and orders "CEASE FIRE-CEASE FIRE" but it is too late. The shell explodes on Gitmo Bay and the General Quarters Alarm was sounded. Then the base sirens goes off, the Air Guard takes to the air and all the ships in the harbor start to get underway. Perhaps Gitmo Bay thinks another Pearl Harbor is ensuing.

After about ten minutes of the mad scramble the CO of the Base opens up on the voice circuit asking "WHO FIRED THAT SHOT?" Each ship in the vicinity gives its call sign and reports: "We did not fire, sir!" The checkoff list continues until all vessels present have answered EXCEPT for the Bassett. The Commandant of the Guantanamo Naval Base directs the Commanding Officer of the USS Bassett to present himself at 0800 tomorrow morning with a full explanation of this event.

Well, a very irritated and embarrassed Captain turns to LT Evans and says: "You will write that letter and have it on my desk 1600 hours today. I intend to take it over today if he will see me. You and your Assistant Gunnery Officer are restricted to the ship and I want those gun crews properly trained starting today!" Well Evans is no Casper Milquetoast and states, "Captain there is nothing wrong with the gun crew. They did exactly what they were instructed to do. The fault lies with an improper command and that lies with me, Sir. You shall have your letter as you have requested."

26

So Evans calls me into the wardroom because I am the Ass't Gun Boss and says: "I'll tell you what Ensign Wren, since we are both confined to the ship this evening, I'll write the first half of the letter to the Commandant for the Skipper if you will write the last half. Is that agreeable?" Well, that seemed like a pretty good arrangement to get the Captain off our backs, so I agreed to the plan. LT Tom Evans took the memo pad and started the letter in standard Navy form:

April 1945

To: Commandant, US Naval Base Guantanamo
From: Commanding Officer, USS Bassett [APD 73]
Subject: Gitmo Bay, The reason we fired on

1. The reason we fired on Guantanamo Bay yesterday is- "Okay", says LT Evans as he hands me the pencil and memo pad. "There is my half! Just finish the sentence and have it prepare for the Captain's signature. Then take it up to his cabin." This was my first lesson in that old Navy axiom--"Never volunteer." Eventually the letter was formulated and typed by the ship's yeoman and delivered to the Captain for his handling. By 0700 the next morning we made sure that his LCVP "Gig" was ready for his trip to the Commandant.

We departed "Gitmo" the same morning when the Captain returned from his visit with the Commandant. The Captain had our new shipping orders in his hands. Nothing more was said except to tell the OOD to set the Special Sea Detail and make preparations to get under way. We made course and speed for the Panama Canal. The fact that we had orders to report to ComSouPac (Commandant South Pacific) may be the reason we got off so easy. We sure did stir up a hornet's nest by that salvo. Some of the crew now brag we won the Battle of Gitmo Bay with one salvo. Maybe they were right.

Rum and Cola

We departed Gitmo Bay enroute to the Panama Canal looking forward to the transit. The Canal was a very busy place and we had heard that the ships had to get in line to go through. We were not a large man of war vessel but we were a ship of the line and we hoped that would help us move through the canal without having to sit out in the hot tropical sun for hours waiting our turn. We were carrying sixty-five Naval pilots who were needed in the Pacific Fleet; surely that would give us some priority! Well, whatever the reason, we had no waiting on the Atlantic side of the Panama Canal.

We cleared the Gatun lock and steamed through Gatun Lake using the fresh waters of the lake to flush our fire main system. Reportedly this helps destroy the barnacles that form on the hull and in the sea intake lines. We passed through the remaining locks of Mira Flores, Pedro Miguel and the large cut in the mountains known as Culebra Pass. At Balboa on the Pacific side of the Canal we stopped to get detached from the Atlantic Fleet and to register with the Pacific Fleet.

The tide on the Pacific side of the Canal is between 30 and 35 feet. When you come into the harbor on high tide your vessel is even with the docks and it is easy to tie up. When the tide drops some 30 odd feet you must tend the lines constantly paying out line until you reach slack tide. When the tide reverses itself you take in the lines as you rise with the incoming tide. You are constantly supervising the handling of the fore and aft mooring lines. In this port the quarterdeck watch has a lot going on in addition to the rise and fall of the tide. When you can get fresh fruit to add to the crew's menu, the Supply Officer always has a work party bringing those stores aboard, no matter what the tide is doing.

Coming through the Canal the Panama work forces handled the lines and the trip was relatively easy. It was then that Doc Pruet decided to show the movies on venereal diseases to all hands. We were called down to the mess hall by divisions and, of course, the junior officers stayed and learned the information along with the men. The movies were informative and you would normally conclude that exposure in most of the seaports was to be avoided. In fact the Doc said that since the Canal had so many foreign vessels traveling through, it would be wise to be extra careful in Balboa if you had liberty and went ashore.

Well, the watch wore on and shortly after the dinner hour a fellow officer offered to take my watch if I wanted to take a stroll into the city. Having had a day full of shifting lines with the tide I accepted his offer and headed out the main gate to have a look at Balboa. Just outside the gate a local bar had a nickelodeon playing the popular song by the Andrew sisters "Rum & Coca Cola" that sounded good and I dropped into the bar to hear the finish of the lyrics. I saddled up to a bar stool and ordered a rum coke. It was just about then that several Panamanian young ladies began to enter the bar area. Perhaps they were the waitresses coming on for the night shift. The barkeeper brought my drink and I paid with a twenty dollar bill which is all I had with me. He came back with the change of nineteen silver dollars and a fifty cent piece suggesting I give the slot machines a try.

Meanwhile, one of which I presumed was a waitresses, slid on to the bar stool next to me. And if I do say so, she had the prettiest lines I had seen all day. She was wearing postage stamps over her ample bosoms and I noted her cleavage was easily revealed in the peek-a-boo garment on her upper body. I didn't glance any lower which I felt was not the proper gentlemanly thing to do. As the nineteen coins clinked and rang on the counter from the barkeepers hands I commented: "The weight of these coins was enough to pull a guy's pants off!" Then this soft speaking brown eyed young lady on the next stool, said to me: "You can get them pulled off for less than that, sailor!"

Well, I had been handling lines all day and now the question was--How was I going to handle the moves she was making with her lines? Taking a large gulp of my drink, I excused myself and headed for the swinging doors. I had been wrestling with tides and lines all day and I didn't plan to get caught up in her mooring lines that evening. I had a slight problem as I made my way back to the Bassett. The slight tilt to the starboard was caused by the silver coins in my right hand pocket. Reflecting on my day in Panama I had seen the Canal with its locks, high and low tides, a small collection of postage stamps, a cleavage line and all of this for fifty cents. The Yankee dollars in my pocket would serve me well in the next port of call.

Leaving Pearl Harbor

The USS Bassett arrived in Pearl Harbor soon after leaving San Diego and was directed to the East Loch for anchorage. The three lochs are the anchorage areas for the "small boys" the DD's, the DE's and the APD's as they are often called. The larger Men of War get the preferred anchoring or docking locations. We had a couple of days training in amphibious tactics and when completed our orders read to report to ComPhilSeaFrontier for further assignment. Also since the war was proceeding northward our camouflaged paint markings were removed and we received a nice fresh coat of battleship grey. All hands noted our new color as we were now just like the big boys. We looked forward to the operations yet to come and doing our part.

When you leave Pearl Harbor the channel takes you past Ford Island where the battleships were anchored. This area is known as Battleship Row. We were able to see the sunken remains of the USS Arizona, a victim of the Pearl Harbor attack. At low tide more of the ship is visible and the fuel oil bubbling up casts a sheen on the water as the morning sun strikes it. As I recall there was a temporary platform placed on the topmost part of the hull on which a flag pole was raised. An American flag was raised to the peak of the flag pole and the colors waved in the morning breeze. The lanyards [lines] for raising and lowering slapped against the metal pole as if chanting "Pray for us!" Then the slapping would cease for a while and the sea gulls would send forth their call as if pleading for us to remember the entombed sailors.

From our bridge the whistle sounds giving us a signal to render honors as we pass to starboard. All hands topside come to attention with a right hand salute as we pass the sunken hull of the USS Arizona. The whistle sounds again and we execute the right hand salute. The sea gulls still call

31

and in the distance the lanyards continue a muffled slapping on the flagstaff. The outgoing tide carries the oil slick seaward as if it is a healing balm which has anointed those below. My eyes cloud up and a tear runs down my face. My prayer goes forth for those entombed and resolve runs through my mind and through my limbs. Many have witnessed this site, few experienced the actual attack, but now the USS Bassett's crew has observed and witnessed the effects; we are deeply touched at the site of the USS Arizona. Departing Pearl Harbor, we are now heading into the forward area of this war.

Faintly now the sea gull continues his call and the lanyards whisper their beat against the flagstaff. The word passes, "Secure the special detail--Set the watch!" The helmsman answers: "Coming left full rudder to course 270, Sir!" We are on our way to our mission and we know why, and we will remember.

There is a special "connection" between the USS Bassett and the USS Arizona of which we knew nothing at this sailing. Later in this book you will learn that LCDR Sam Fuqua of the USS Arizona will give his daughter in marriage to LT Charles Nagle one of the skippers of the Bassett in WWII. LCDR Fuqua was the recipient of the Congressional Medal of Honor for his brave action aboard the Arizona during the Pearl Harbor attack.

Imperium Neptuni Regis
Crossing the Equator Ceremony

The USS Bassett is steaming south for the port of Hollandia, New Guinea and operating independently as we search the waters for Japanese submarines along this well traveled course. The old salts, "shellbacks," have been planning carefully for this occasion for a proper initiation of the "pollywogs" aboard. By definition a shellback is a sailor who has crossed the equator from North to South. A pollywog has not yet made this transit. On 14 June 1945 we automatically became members of the "Golden Dragon Domain" when we crossed the 180 degree longitude. This passing is like a lull before a storm as the shellbacks wait and plot against those who can't find their official card indicating they have crossed the equator before and must submit to the Kings Court for dereliction of duty along with all the new pollywogs. On 10 July 1945 we will cross the equator and King Neptune's crew looks forward to greeting us. We have been advised by ComDesPac {Commander Destroyer Pacific Fleet} that hard hazing would not be tolerated but then ComDesPac doesn't know some of our ingenious shellbacks.

This is the day and it starts out with all pollywogs wearing their uniforms backwards. You talk about fun and laughter in trying to help someone else put his uniform on backwards and then he discovers he has to answer a mother nature call. All pollywogs off duty are assembled before the Royal Court on the fantail, and stripped to their under shorts. All pollywog officers must wear their black tie and have it properly two blocked up to the Adams Apple of their neck. All pollywogs are issued an unshelled peanut and told to push it by their nose around the deck on a designated course. Those who don't keep in line are encouraged to do so by a wallop of a stocking filled with rags. Nothing to hurt you but startling to say the least. Those who are too speedy getting around the course are given a wallop to slow them down, while those who are laying back too far are given a wallop to hasten them to close the gap. When the pollywogs reach to what appears to be the end of the course they are hit with a powerful spray from the salt water fire hose which just about washes them over the side. Along with the stocking wallops the pollywogs are addressed with such nautical terms as "Scupper Slime", Wharf Rat, and "Slimey Snail" to encourage their continued nose pursuit of the peanut around the deck. If you lose your peanut when the salt water hose hits you, you are chastited and made to crawl into the court of King Neptune. The king is always the fattest guy on the ship whose bare belly is covered with foamy shaving cream and your face and head are unceremoniously shoved into his fat belly. This was known as kissing the "Royal Pudding!"

From here the pollywog goes to the Royal Barber to be tidied up for King Neptune's Ball. The barber takes a couple of good size patches of hair off the back of his head. Now the pollywog is directed to enter the King's chamber on his knees as he proceeds to the King's Ball. This is a target sleeve about ten feet long and three foot in diameter filled with the garbage that has been saved for about a week in the hot sun in a GI can. With the encouragement of a few wallops the pollywog is plunged into this mess; needless to say he will hurry through it. Upon his exit he is hit again with the salt water fire hose which again nearly knocks him over the side. This ends the initiation and the new shellback is now part of King Neptune's Domain. Now the next group starts the peanut pushing deck tour while those who have completed their initiation relieve those on watch who have yet to be welcomed into King Neptune's Domain. The Supply Officer ends the ceremony for all hands when he issues chocolate nut sundaes.

I hope all you Bassett shellbacks have carefully saved your King Neptune ID cards because the ship's cook I know,

Earle Houghtaling by name, says he enjoys saving garbage for special occasions.

Hollandia Village - New Guinea

Native Village
Hollandia, New Guinea

We have just dropped the port anchor in Hollandia Harbor, New Guinea and are awaiting the next assignment of convoy duty. We are below the equator in southern latitudes and have completed our King Neptune Rex ceremonies. With the ceremony we have erased the pollywogs from our crew and now stand ready to serve Neptune Rex with a strong crew of "shellbacks." Believe me the ship's cook "did himself proud" in collecting the weeks garbage which we so nauseously crawled through. Thank God for the fire main hose wash off, although it almost swept you over the side.

Lt(jg) Anderson, using his binoculars located a native village on the edge of a small river. Lt(jg) Anderson invited me to join Ensign Leweke and Chief Desmond and him on a trip to visit this village. The village sat on stilts above the river bed, and he believed we could get to it by walking along the water's edge. Two feet into the jungle from the water's edge was heavily ladened in tropical growth. A man could easily get lost if he didn't stay close to the water's edge. As we got to the river's edge where it joined the rolling surf of the ocean we saw local natives fishing in the stream; through sign language were able to bum a ride on their outriggers to the stilted village. Mind you now, Ensign Leweke and I are 6'2" and each weigh about 200 lbs.

When we got into that outrigger the freeboard distance dropped to about one-half inch. The freeboard is the area from the waterline to the top of the outriggers canoe side. The native waved us on as to say, "don't worry this craft is seaworthy" I expected us to ship water but we never did. Our native had only a left hand and with his right arm stump from the wrist up he pulled on the paddle while the left hand controlled the paddle. When we landed near the ladder to climb up to the platform of the village, he held the canoe close to the ladder to make our climb easy. It was then, by sign language, I asked what had happened to his right hand. By gesture he indicated that the Japanese troops had invaded the village and had cut off the right hands of all men who could throw a spear or shoot a gun. The young people of the village were taken away for slave labor, and all that remained were elderly grandmothers and very young children. The village had neat rows of cottages built from logs which lined the main planked road. At the end of the planks stood a hut with a small steeple and a christian cross over the door. It appeared Dutch missionaries helped establish this village. The natives were pleasant and courteous to us and we of course were the same to them. We had brought some ID chains, some beads, and a nice brass lock to trade with them. They had little to trade and graciously tuned down our offer to trade. Below the stilts were several peccary (wild boars) which they were raising. The women were modestly clothed and the men wore only a loin cloth.

We are very near to the equator and the sun is beastly hot. We had not planned well for this trip and did not have any water to drink. The children, in most cases, under 6 years of age, ran around in their birthday suits and played just like all children do. We indicated to our native canoers that we would like to go back across the river. This time we split up the weight in the out-riggers and the freeboard was now about 2" above the water line. Going back I trailed my hands in the water and wiped some on my face. My canoe was a hollowed out log about 12" in diameter and I must sit with each cheek of my butt resting on the narrow side rail. Trailing my hands in the river water causes the native to direct me to keep my hands inside of the canoe log as there are piranha in these waters and I could lose a finger if not a hand. I thanked him then and again when we landed on the beach. The trip to the boat landing was uneventful. When we got back the ship, the water coming from the scuttlebutt never tasted better.

The next morning just after "Muster on Station" we had several native "bum boats" along side. The local male natives paddle these out rigger canoes out to the ships where the local women natives try to trade their local crafts to the sailors. A large brightly clothed native woman is calling out, "Hey sailor boy, you got trade?" Her trade was a carved coconut shell and what she wanted was a sailors mattress cover. This is a six foot piece of cotton cloth that covers the sailor's mattress. Usually every sailor has two of them-one in use and one in reserve. The local natives are able to color the cloth with local native dies and they wear them as a dress. The native women trying to trade is wearing a bright yellow one. I have the Quarter Deck watch and so I shoo her away from the gangway. She continues to work toward the stern on the opposite side of the Quarter Deck. In observing her I notice that she has these bloody red juices running down her chin and I learned from others that she is chewing the "betel nut". This is a nut that acts as 'pep up pill' and does generate a bloody red saliva. Later when I heard the music and lyrics of "South Pacific" I readily understood the character "Bloody Mary" who is always chewing "betel nut". We had not met formally but "Bloody Mary" is a character I will never forget.

Atolls--Gab-Gab

The Bassett had been busy with convoy and escort duty and would soon be grouping up to make the run north to Tokyo Bay as all operations were beamed that way. Meanwhile to keep morale high we were ordered to the recreational areas in the South Pacific. These areas were located on different atolls in the Pacific on which beaches and a baseball diamonds were established. In steaming for these atolls which are hardly above sea level, we found if you steered in the general direction of your base course toward the low lying clouds, you would find the atolls very easily. The clouds seemed to form over the vegetation of the land masses.

I have no idea who was in charge of naming these recreational spots but whoever he was, he must have been working with a local native who had a very limited vocabulary. For example, we had one area called "Gab-Gab" and one named "Mog-Mog." You will have to agree these would not be a very descriptive names to write about when you dropped line to mother as to where you were hanging out in the South Pacific. Surely when she received your communication she would call on her local priest seeking his help to get her darling boy home before he becomes any more "looney" than his letters indicate. If her local priest couldn't help her I'm sure the "Red Cross Agency" would receive a worried mother's visitation seeking their help. Other names that have been added to our vocabulary are Ulithi and Eniwetok, better known as "You-like-it-here" and "Any-wee-talk." No doubt your mother will think you have gone bananas out here and will never come home the same as you left.

In making these three "B" (beach, baseball and beer) morale trips we were loaded up with two cans of 3.2 beer per crew member but there would always be a question of

39

procedure. Should we play baseball first and then have a warm beer after a swim or should we have the cold beer now and play ball later? A vote would be taken and the results always came out about the same. Half wanted the cold beer now and the rest wanted the ball game first. The discussion served as a good mixer for each of the ship's divisions to know each other better. The discussions were always colorful as the Engineer gang (Snipes) would challenge the Deck gang (Deck Apes) who would challenge the gun crews (Gunneys) who would challenge the Bridge gang (Skivvy Wavers). Junior Officers were assigned to be the chaperones (think referee) on these occasions. As for me, I went for a swim on the beach and donated my beers to the bakers with the thought that it might help when I am on the Mid-watch. The smell of freshly baked bread permeated the bridge area at night. Bakers worked the ovens at night while the cooks had them during the day. It sure would be tasty to have a heel of freshly baked bread or a cinnamon bun to munch on at two in the morning.

The beers that the recreational department supplied always had unknown or strange names like Old Griesdieck, Iron City or Old Pitt. We had some colorful names for them which I cannot put into print but I am sure you can figure out the slang names. It was always good to get off the ship for a while. We always enjoyed these three "B" breaks from the monotony of shipboard routine.

The Marianas Islands

The following is given to help the reader's understanding of this area of the Pacific Ocean. Because of the ten small islands extending from the larger three islands, the Spanish Jesuit missionary priests named these island the "Marianas". They reminded the priests of a decade of the rosary. The rosary is a beaded prayer asking the Blessed Mother to intercede for the praying person with the Lord.

The Spanish governed these islands from 1668 until 1898. After the Spanish American War the Spanish claims to the islands were released, and the United States took the large island of Guam as a protectorate and established a US Naval base there. The rest of the islands were sold to Germany by Spain.

In WWII Japan captured the Island of Guam December 10, 1941. The US Naval Forces held out as long as they could but finally had to surrender. However three sailors, one of which was a radioman escaped into the jungle and continued to supply information on Japanese ship movement to American Forces. Two of the sailors were eventually captured but the radioman continued giving information on Japanese troop movements. The US Armed forces recaptured Guam in August 1944. At that time the radioman walked out of the jungle and to the surprise of his American shipmates, he looked more like Robinson Crusoe than a sailor. The loyal native Guam people hid him when the Japanese were getting close to capturing him.

The Marianas Island chain is the eastern boundary of the Philippine Sea and the Philippine Islands serve as the western boundary. About 1100 miles is the distance across this sea and the Indianapolis was believed to be sunk about half way across

Guam became a naval base again and the Islands of Saipan and Tinian, after some wicked fighting became links in

41

the chain of islands as the US Forces moved north toward Tokyo. The island of Rota was bypassed because it had little value for military needs. Tinian had a level plain and with US Construction Battalions (think Sea Bees) help, it became an American Air Base.

It was to Tinian that the atomic bomb parts were delivered by the USS Indianapolis for the planned bombing of Hiroshima on 6 August 1945. A medical hospital was established on Guam and was the final site for medical help of the Indianapolis survivors The USS Bassett which received its orders from the Philippine Sea Frontier brought its 152 survivors to the Philippine Island Samar Medical Facility. The Samar Medical Facility was reputed to be able to handle about 3000 patients. The other rescue ships which helped in the rescue proceeded to the Peleliu Medical Facility. Later all the survivors were transferred to the Guam Medical Hospital.

When the Bassett arrived at midnight on the 3rd of August 1945 there were no other ships on the Bassett's radar screen, according to Lt[jg] Ralph Horwitz--CIC officer on the Bassett.

By 6:00 am on August 3rd the sea area was full of ships to aid the survivors. Dr Harlan A. Stiles was transferred from the USS Madison (DD 425) to assist the Bassett's Dr Royce Pruet. With two medical doctors and two pharmacist mates aboard, the Bassett departed for Samar Island at 6:00 am. The author who was taking a break while the survivors were being unloaded from the LCVP's, greeted Dr Stiles at about 4:20 am as he landed on the Bassett's deck via the boatswains chair swung from the bow of the USS Madison.

Manila 1945

From Leyte we were ordered to Manila Bay, as the war moved north we traveled by the inland sea among all the various islands which comprise the Philippine Islands. Luzon is the largest of the many islands and the seat of the government. As we enter Manila Bay we pass the Island of Corregidor where our troops held out as long as they could and finally surrendered to the Japanese in December 1941. We passed the Bataan Peninsula where the captured American troops started their Bataan Death March. We proceed into the Manila Bay Harbor, and the chart provided by the US Hydrographic Office of Washington, DC shows clearly our designated anchorage circle; however it does not show the number of sunken ships enroute to our anchorage. Some ships we can easily see because their masts and smoke stacks are above water. But there are many we find with our lead line. The Bassett draws 16 feet of water at the bow and slightly more at the stern. To be sure we are in deep enough water we station the boatswain mate at the bow of the ship and he throws out a line to determine the depth. His line carries different markers and he sings out the specific marker he sees when the lead strikes the bottom. It is like the "old time" navy entering a strange harbor and the skill should not be lost.

For safety sake we require four fathoms [24 feet] under the bow. If less than this we reverse our engines, back down and try another course. Our sonar dome for "echo ranging" on enemy submarines hangs below the ships hull and we don't want to damage it. Eventually we reach our anchorage and drop the "hook" as we call our anchor. The job is not done until we have checked a round of bearings making sure we are not drifting if the anchor is not holding. Entering a war time harbor is a tricky maneuver. We are moving up the island chains and our Captain reports to

COMPHILSEAFRONTIER for our next assignment. All anchor details seem secure, so the next thing is a chance to stretch our legs on the beach.

We catch the first "Liberty Launch" and make our way carefully around the sunken vessels to the harbor docks. Ashore we find the ravages of war on a city which once was a gem in the Pacific. We find the Filipinos trying to eke out a living from their war torn country; the most enterprising ones have set up little stalls in front of bombed out buildings and stores. There is not much merchandise of interest and the main item seems to be food. One of the foods being offered was enough to kill any luncheon appetite. One stall was boiling earth worms and offering a plate of them for a small amount of cash. At this point I refer you to Ensign Mal Smook's letter to his family. Mal's family had lived in Manila prior to the war and he served as our guide in touring the area. Mal has given me permission to reproduce part of his letter to his family and it describes well our "Manila" encounter.

Ltr from Ensign Mal Smook
Thursday 6 September 1945

Dear Mom and Boys:

Yesterday, I had a thrilling experience. I walked up the Royal Avenue, on the Escolts, and crossed the Jones Bridge. I even took a turn up Dewey Boulevard. Yes, we anchored in Manila Bay, and the best of, all censorship has been relaxed so I can tell you all about it.

We came in two days ago, but I had the duty the first day and I couldn't get away, Yesterday Pete Wren and Chuck Nagle, two of the other officers on the ship and I, went into town to see all we could. I was to act in the capacity of guide.

First the harbor is a mess of sunken ships just about where the "Pathfinder" used to anchor. We can count two dozen super structures and hulls alone protruding from the water right near our own ship. The fleet landing (for small boats) is in the river right under the Jones Bridge. The bridge itself took a bomb hit and the middle portion has been repaired with a steel structure. The city itself is in unbelievable shape. Only one building in ten in the downtown area is in usable shape, and some escaped unscathed. The merchants, if you can call them as such, now live in hovels made from the wreckage. The downtown section has stalls built into the bombed out store fronts of the buildings and everyone is out for the sailor's money. Nearly all of the stalls that exist sell either native whiskey or souvenirs. I am enclosing some Japanese printed centavos (for the boys) that are being sold as souvenirs.

It didn't take the Filipinos long to find out they could charge the American sailor anything they chose. You don't hear the word "centavos." It is nothing but "peso," one peso or five pesos A plate of ham and eggs is four dollars (not pesos). Whiskey is a dollar a glass, and chickens, of all things, are eight dollars a piece.

We thought the way to get around town would be in a "Caromata." Those robbers now ask and get between five and seven and a half dollars an hour just to drive aimlessly through and around town. Needless to say, we thought the walk would do us good.

After seeing the downtown district, we set out for Dewey Boulevard. We saw the walled city and only about one-tenth stands now. The Manila Hotel has been fairly well repaired and is one of the few buildings standing. We walked by the edge of the ArmyNavy Club swimming pool and I saw the platform that I crawled off on my hand and knees. Then we looked for the Reidell Boarding House. Not even a reminant remains of it or the Rogers House next door. Troops have pitched tents in the area where the first line of houses used to be. They are so completely demolished, I easily could have missed the old site. An old stomping ground that I did find however, was the Gaiety. It looked like it hadn't done business since the last Hoot Gibson movie we saw, but the name was still attached to the battle scarred front.

We will be leaving here in a day or so and I will try to write soon. There is still no news in new orders and getting home. All my love to you and the rest of the family.

/s/ Malcom

Nagoya, Japan

The war had ended on 15 August 1945 and shortly after our HECP duty at Wakayama, Japan we were ordered to Nagoya for HECP duty. This is an assignment to help ships entering that harbor by providing corrected charts indicating where the shipping channels are cleared of mines. Some of the mines were ours in addition to those the Japanese had installed to protect their coastal ports. Harbor Entrance Control Posts are busy assignments and ideal for APDs as we can easily send any of our four LCVPs to deliver the corrected navigational charts for the ship entering that harbor. It was interesting to note that the charts we were using were from the Hydrographic Office of Washington, D.C. with Japanese characters on them along with our English language. I can't recall the date on the bottom corner of the maps.

In going ashore in Japan we were instructed that the war was over and not to take or attempt to take any vengeance on the local people. Most of us felt we didn't have to be told this and were surprised at our reception upon landing. The Japanese greeting us were the "momma-sans" and the "poppa-sans" and the small children. Those Japanese of warring ages were nowhere in sight. The grandmothers and grandfathers bowed graciously to us while the children danced, smiled and were great ambassadors making us feel welcome. None of us could resist the cute happy children. When the grandparents saw our reaction to the children, smiles and greetings emanated from the visitors and the locals. My friend Colonel Lewis I. Held, US Army, of Richmond Virginia who was on General MacArthur's Staff in Tokyo told me when he was enroute from Tokyo to Osaka, the Japanese they met on the road would turn their backs to the convoy as it passed because they were so embarrassed. They didn't have the little children to lead them as we did.

While performing our HECP duties we observed a Japanese fishing boat coming out of the harbor and apparently with the throttle wide open and heading for our US WARSHIPS swinging on the hook [at anchor] in the area. We challenged them by flashing light with no recognition whatsoever. So we called away our number one "boarding party". With the LCVP underway in their direction with several hand guns beamed in their direction, they didn't seem to want to yield. Once the salvo from the five inch gun splashed off their bow we saw their stern raise up from the water as they cut their speed. Expert rifle men drawing a bead on their small crew were not surprised to see their arms go up "Cowboy Style". We figured they knew enough sign language from watching our Western Movies. The boarding party went aboard and found nothing but fishing gear; and strongly suggested they return to harbor. When the boarding party got back aboard the Boatswain mate informed the OOD that he had scratched the fish off the Blue Plate luncheon for that day. We transmitted our findings to the Port Control and received a "Well Done" We did not witness this type of incident again while we had the HECP duty at Nagoya.

It was while we were in the harbor that a typhoon struck the area. We had put out both the port and starboard anchors and were steaming at full speed ahead with one engine on the line and were still dragging toward the beach. At that time I was the First Lieutenant aboard the Bassett and had been instructed to let out more chain in hopes it would prevent us from dragging on the beach. Several ships in our area were requesting tugboats to prevent them from going aground. We had rigged heavy duty lines forward and with a minimum crew we were out on the fos'cle, hanging on for dear life, as we paid out anchor chain to each anchor. It was then I looked up toward the bridge in the pelting wind and rain and I realized I could not only see the bridge but could see our depth charges on the fantail. This statement should give the reader an idea of the force of a typhoon. I remember praying, "Oh God, your ocean is so large and our ship is so small!"

The date of this event took place on I October 1945. Had the war not ended when it had on August 15, 1945, the American Naval Forces would have been grouped up and heading for the southern most Island of the Japan. Our Naval Forces would had to endure this typhoon just a few weeks before the "D" Day of 1 November 1945.

It is interesting to note that in previous Japanese history when the Chinese War Lords were warring against Japan the Chinese encountered a similar typhoon off Kyushu. When the storm had passed there was no Chinese Fleet. Of course then the ships were of wood using sail power. The Island of Kyushu was awash with boat timbers and drowned Chinese warriors. It has been told that the Japanese were praying for their Shinto Gods to deliver this type on storm on the American Fleet should they approach their homeland. Since the Bassett was scheduled to make that landing on or about 1 November 1945, I doubt I, like my shipmates listed herein, would be around to tell this story.

Sasebo, Japan
21 November 1945

When we arrive at Sasebo, Japan I drew the Shore Patrol Duty that all junior officers are always enthused about. [Can we have a "Bravo Sierra" here!] It gets you off the ship from routine duties with a chance to get the lay of the land in the new port. Our duty was limited to the dock areas so we were not quite into meeting the local gentry. In a war torn area poverty is very pronounced.

Near the harbor landings where our LCVPs would ferry the ship's crews from ship to shore, there were several large warehouses. One in particular had a lot of "coming and going" activity and upon checking it out we learned the warehouse had a large cache of Japanese rifles and swords. Someone was issuing them as souvenirs and fortunately for me one of the men in my division brought me a sample of each. I boxed up the rifle and sent it home via the US Mail but it never arrived. I hope some worthy person is enjoying the "nine mm barrel" that never made it home. The sword I have with me to this date.

Another warehouse contained a large community pool where families were coming to bathe. Mothers, father and children would careful wash at the side of the pools and then all would immerse themselves in the pools after they had washed and rinsed off on the sides of the pool using small buckets. Every one was very discrete and in my observation of this family function, found me equally as discrete, respecting this family custom.

On the next day when relieved of the Shore Patrol Duty, we were told we could go up the Nagasaki area that received the "atomic bomb" but not to go past the area patrolled by the sentry. On this trip ashore I had gone alone. I walked through this waterfront community, well outside of the range of the atomic bomb, and found it was composed of small frame houses with store operations on the lower level and living quarters on the second level. Nothing was over two stories high. Japanese children played in the streets under the watchful eye of the "momma-sans" and again the smiles, and sing song of the children brought smiles to all faces as we passed to see the damaged area.

It didn't take long to get the souvenir business underway with "Sailor Sam" and "GI Joe" visiting the small shops. The favorite trade items for the "GI" was either "chocolato" (hershey bar) or "cigaretto" (American cigarettes) with bargaining back and forth with the "momma-san." Our military script was acceptable but they, much preferred the "greenback Dollars". Standard operation was for the ship's Supply Officer to recapture all your green dollars when we left Pearl Harbor. We received an equivalent amount of military script dollars which we could spend on the ship's or the various recreational facilities established by the US Government. The local Japanese did not want to get stuck with the "Military Script" as their local banks weren't sure about it's redemption. There were a few of the crew who had the green dollars and their trades were with plus values. As our days continued in port and with each added day it seemed better souvenirs were beginning to appear from the local family stores.

It has been fifty-four years since I made this walk into the atomic bombed area and I am not quite sure if my visit was from our anchorage near Kure which is very close to Hiroshima or my visit originated from the Sasebo anchorage. The bombed areas covered quite a large land mass and the areas were still radiating harmful rays. Our Armed Forces would be standing guard well away from the centers of the bomb site. The scientists would be the only persons permitted a closer view. My memory recalls the walk to see the area of the atomic bomb. I was met by the sentry who reaffirmed, "you could look all you wanted, but not one step further than the designated markers!" My view was that of a very flat open piece of land with stubble strewn everywhere and a large cement building which seemed about 10 to 15 miles away. There were acres of three stair steps leading up to a foundation of a home. Quite often an iron radiator would appear within the foundation area. As I looked further toward what I presumed to be the center no shape or form was discernible, just rubble. From the sentry's position, there were acres and acres of stair stoops that broke down into rubble This area could have been a comfortable residential area. The sun shone brightly that day in November 1945. There was not a tree, nor a bush, nor a blade of grass, nor a weed and absolute silence prevailed. The site was awesome and the only sound I heard was my occasional sigh as I reflected on the three stair stoops that led to, I'm sure, happy homes. Here was another site like that of the USS Indianapolis. Loved ones were now gone. No farewell. No remains to carefully lay to rest. Just a memory for those who survived. Thank God for the atomic bomb as it ended this war. What would it have been like if we had to invade the Island of Kyushu and fight our way, stoop by stoop, to Tokyo. We would be making orphans of those happy children I had just past down the street. "Lord," I prayed, "let us give peace a chance. Let all nations come and see and understand this leveled field!"

Fresh Water

When I researched the USS Bassett's 1945 logs prior to going to the 1997 Reunion, I found that the injection temperature was listed as 85 degrees. This is the heat of the water we bring into the ship to make steam. Once the steam is made it is routed to the generators to make electrical current, to the propulsion turbines to propel the ship and to the evaporators to make fresh water. This temperature does not conflict with the report Doc Haynes gave saying the water was about 11 degrees below normal body temperature, (98.6 minus 11 degrees equals 87 degrees.) Since the salt seawater comes into the ship at the bottom of the ship the temperature at sea level could be two degrees higher.

Salt in a water solution acts like a purgative. This causes a rapid transfer of food and fluids through the GI tract, thus diarrhea. This is because the salt water is much more concentrated than your body fluids. Obviously this would magnify dehydration. This is further complicated by the fact that the heart pumps faster to help you cool off through perspiration. A long time in this warm water saps your strength. The body needs to be well hydrated to handle the stress and physical demands. When hydration suffers, your performance suffers physically and mentally. Hence this can contribute to hallucinations or altered mental status. The sun's exposure also increases fluid loss. The loss of blood from wounds and the excrement from diarrhea attracts sharks. One thing compounds the other. It is like the old Aesop fable for the want of a nail the shoe was lost and for the want of a shoe the horse was lost, and so forth until we lose the battle for life. Thus the survivors of the USS Indianapolis clung to life by a fingernail, until help could get there.

The fresh water report is read every day with the eye kept on its usage. Because fresh water is so important to our well being at sea we must have an adequate supply at all times. It is the steam driving the gears of the generators that makes the electrical current flow to the gyros, the lighting, the steering, the electrical stoves, and most of all the guns that must train, elevate and shoot. And finally it is the steam that is cooled for our potable water which is the source of our cooking, bathing, drinking and laundry. If there is any shortage then the ship's crew and Officers go on "water hours" until the evaporators can generate enough for all needs.

Quietly the engineering gang produced the fresh water needed while others washed and poured liquids into those in greatest need. In the hot South Pacific no one likes "water hours" which means the showers are available on a very limited basis. Those of the Bassett crew who were actually working with the survivors whether lifting them out of the ocean, or bringing them aboard, or on the wash detail cleaning them up were getting as oil covered as the survivors. So we had about one half of our crew of 192 plus the 152 survivors all in need of fresh water. Our Chief Engineer Ltjg William Anderson cranked up the production of the evaporators to answer that need. The engineering department though hidden from view were as important to the survivors recovery as those topside actually handling the survivors. A thank you and "Well Done" is in order for the Engineering Department.

Souvenir Hunting-Nagoya, Japan
November 1945

When the Japanese surrendered in August 1945 they were not sure how the American troops would treat them in the planned occupation of their homeland. But barriers were soon broken in spite of language difficulties as the local nationals eagerly traded souvenirs for the American cigarettes [cigaretto] and candy bars [chocolato]. The better souvenirs were hidden and what was being offered in 1945 at the LCVP boat landings was similar to what we already had in our local Five and Dime stores in the United States. Sailor Sam and Seaman Deuce wanted something better and so the search was on to add to their souvenir collections.

Opportunity presented itself while we were swinging on the hook [anchored] off of Nagoya, Japan. The Bassett's boat coxswains while making the "Liberty Trips" to the Nagoya boat landing noticed a seemingly abandoned airfield with hangars and other buildings just off the river running into Nagoya Bay. So Sailor Sam and Seaman Deuce got thinking that if they could find a way to get to these hangars or buildings there might be some interesting souvenirs available. About eight guys, we will call them the "Running Eight," came up with a plan. It was simple. They would convince a boat coxswain he could benefit from their search as a full partner but he had to help them get into position to capture the suspected treasures. The coxswain would run the Nagoya "Liberty" trip but let the "running eight" off at the airfield. On the early return trip from the Nagoya landing he usually carried no passengers back to the ship, so he would then go by the airfield and wait for the "running eight" while they explored the air base.

Well one day the "running eight" boarded an LCVP and headed out on their mission and with the boat coxswain's help they made their landing on the airfield and proceeded

55

rapidly for the hangars. Cautiously they entered the hangars being mindful of "Booby" traps or possible guards on watch. Nothing and no one seemed to impede their progress. Inside the hangar they found tools, aircraft parts and two disabled airplanes over which they climbed. They picked up tools and other items that had Japanese name plates on them. Others were trying to get parts off the planes dash boards which had Japanese writing on them. They were having a ball. They thought they had struck the "mother lode" of souvenirs. Suddenly someone shouted: "MPs on the way!" Now you learn why they were called the "running eight." With hands full of various items, they took off like it was the quarter mile sprint in the Olympics for the LCVP waiting for them. The MPs got to the river bank to watch the LCVP's wake wash up on the bank.

Smiling all the way back to the Bassett the fun of the chase was worth more than the captured souvenirs, The MPs did not get the boat number on the LCVP so there were some questions raised about an unauthorized visit to an airfield. However the questions were never answered. This just proves that the "running eight" was a running group and not a talking group. However if you ever get to visit Jack Paul he will gladly show you his Japanese rifle he got from Sasebo, Japan, but you have to ask to see the box of miscellaneous souvenirs that just sits on a shelf in the closet. They are useless except for the memories and he just "jogs" these days.

Chapter Two

An overview of the rescue by the Bassett and the Oral histories of the USS Bassett Crew

Bassett to the Rescue

On Station D in the Philippine Sea the USS Bassett on August 2, 1945 continues to search and sweep seeking the enemy submarines that probe this area. Small talk goes on as the watch sometimes seems boring. The JOOD, Junior watch Officer, mentions: "that the Philippine Sea which is between the Marianas Islands and the Philippines Islands has the deepest trough in the Pacific Ocean. If you are going to get sunk this is not the place if you expect to have your ship recovered." While this small talk ensues very few know that the atomic bomb has already been delivered to Tinian on 26 July 1945 and will be dropped on Hiroshima just four days from now. The only thing that can stop the bomb is for the Japanese War Powers to agree with the Potsdam Declarations. At the conclusion of the war in Europe the Germans agreed to an unconditional surrender and Japan is asked to do the same. President Harry Truman, Prime Minister Winston Churchill and Premier Josef Stalin met in Potsdam and established the rules for surrender.

The bomb parts delivered by the Indy consisted of the firing mechanism which was a 15 foot crate bolted down to the deck and two lead containing cylinders weighing about two hundred pounds each lashed down in the Flag Officers quarters. Two army officers, a Major Robert R. Fuhrman and a Captain James F. Nolan escort the devices for the trip to Tinian and both are posing as Artillery Officers. The secret of the cargo is known only by the escorting officers and they do not share this information with Captain Charles B. McVay III. The marine guards stand watch on the firing mechanism bolted to the deck and the Artillery Officers have the lead canisters under their surveillance in the Flag Officer's stateroom.

The USS Bassett steaming as before, receives an urgent message on Wednesday 2nd August 1945 at 1450

58

hours to "proceed with best speed to latitude 11 degrees 34 minutes north latitude and 133 degrees 47 minutes East Longitude to search for survivors of an unknown origin." The message was dated 02 August 1945 at 0502 hours. By dead reckoning we estimated we could be at the position by 0030 navy time. We sighted a life raft at 0052 am and had our three boats in the water by 0056. Ltjg Ralph Horwitz advised that there were no other ships on the radar scope, so we thought we were the first to arrive. By the ship's log of the USS Doyle they had arrived at 0015. We had our first survivors aboard the Bassett at 0121 hours.

Checking on the information available from ships' logs it is known that the USS Doyle was the first rescue ship to the scene. Herewith is a listing of arrivals.

Ship Name	Arrival date/time		Rescued.
USS DOYLE DE386	Fri 3 Aug'45	0015	93
USS BASSETT APD73	Fri 3 Aug'45	0052	152
USS DUFILHO DE 423	Fri 3 Aug'45	0300	1
USS MADISON DD425	Fri 3 Aug'45	0400	0
USS TALBOT DE 390	Fri 3 Aug'45	0500	24
USS RINGNESS APD 100	Fri 3 Aug'45	1025	39
USS REGISTER APD 92	Fri 3 Aug'45	1045	12

At 0600am on the 3rd of August the Bassett, observing other ships now on the scene, advised ComPhilSeaFrontier that we were departing the rescue scene with about 200 survivors, most of whom were stretcher cases. We set course for the Samar Medical Facility at full speed and estimated we would make landfall on Samar by 0800am on the 4th of August. The captain felt the other ships could recover the balance of survivors, if any, in the daylight hours. The survivors aboard the Bassett needed more immediate help than our medical staff could provide.

At 1400 hours CDR Todd of the USS Madison and Senior Officer Present Afloat [SOPA] directed rescue operations and ordered the Dufilho and Talbot to transfer their survivors to the USS Register which now would have 37 survivors. The USS Doyle was released to take its survivors to Peleliu Medical Facility and to return for continued search duty. (See Chapter five search plans).

Ltr from James D. Arthur WT3/c
crew member of USS Bassett

December 1998

Dear Peter:

Thank God I am feeling better now and will be able to jot down a few remarks as I remember them concerning the rescuing of the survivors of the USS Indianapolis.

I was a Watertender third class on the USS Bassett. Due to the fact that my duty station was down below the main deck in #1 fireroom, I am lacking in first hand information. As I recall it was on a Sunday just after noon that I was topside in a beautiful sun while we were patrolling out of Leyte. All at once our ship made a sudden 45 degree turn to the right and picked up speed. We all began to look for subs and none could be located. I went down to the #1 fireroom to learn what was taking place but they didn't know. Soon the captain came on the PA system and said that we have orders to pick up survivors at a certain point.

We traveled until just after midnight when we reached the scene. I was told that the boat crew, on the first LCVP that was put into the water, were given orders to demand of the survivors three American names for identification. The first name the survivors gave was the Indianapolis. This was the first time that it was known that the USS Indianapolis was sunk.

We were all at Battle Quarters during the rescue mission. The boat crews are to be praised in the laborious task of rescuing. I was told there were 149 men, 3 officers and one deceased and one we lost after he was brought aboard. I did get a short view of the pitiful task of bringing the survivors aboard--so sad. After we had picked up a ship's load of survivors we headed for the hospital on the island of Samar. We arrived there the next day and anchored in the inlet near the island. I had gone topside to get a jug of water for our watch section below in #1 fireroom when I saw a line of Red Cross ambulances on the land that could have been one-half mile long. The hospital sent out barges which tied up along side the Bassett. I was surprised to see how many survivors could maneuver themselves while others had to be taken off by stretchers. By the time we reached Samar the survivors had been cleaned up with diesel oil and placed in bunks of troop quarters topside. After serving my four hour watch, I came out of the fire room hatch and took a few steps into the survivors quarters. On my right, a few bunks in was a sailor on his side with one eye swollen shut. I was always curious to know where their homes were and I said to him, "Where are you from?" He replied in a slow voice: "Logansport." I said, "Indiana?" He said, "Are you from Indiana?" I replied, "Yes." He raised up a little and stuck out his hand and said, "Put it there!" I asked him if he would like some juice to drink which the medical officer aboard had issued orders to give them all they would take. There was only pear juice left and I asked him if he would like some. He responded, "Yes, I would," and I got him some. We talked some and even about a Baptist minister who often entertained 4H kids as a magician. When we ran out of things to talk about he said to me, "Let's talk about girls a little!" I thought in my own mind-"man, after all you have been through." I told him I was a married man with two daughters, one a teenager, and I did not know much about girls. He replied, " I don't either but I like to tease my wife!"

After we had returned home my family and I attended a football game at Purdue and on the way home my son in law said to me, "Granddad, you have never looked up that survivor-McVay." I told my son-in-law to stop at the telephone booth down on the corner and I would try to locate him. I looked in the book and there were about seven McVays listed. I had forgotten his first name but I thought I would try one. A lady answered the phone and I told her I was looking for the McVay that was a survivor of the USS Indianapolis. She said, "You have the right place and my husband is here. Would you like to talk to him?" He came on the phone and I told him who I was and that I had fed him some pear juice one time but he wouldn't remember it. When I told him I was off the USS Bassett he asked, "Where in the world are you?" I said," Downtown on the corner." He then asked me: "Where are you going?" I said," To our daughters in Kokomo." "You are going right close to our house and you have got to stop and see me!" So we did. We drove up to his house and there he was waiting for us. He grabbed my wife and kissed her and then came around and greeted me and the rest of us. He said," I want you to come in, sit down and tell me everything you know." I began to relate how I knew him and the different things we talked about. I came to the place where I ran out of things to say and where he said to me," Let's talk about girls!'" He threw his hands up into the air and said to his wife across the room," That's me!" His name is Richard C. McVay, Yeoman 3/c. I said to him, "One time that name McVay didn't hurt did it?" He said: "No!" with a grin. "I was in Captain McVay's Quarters most of the time." {Note: Captain Charles B. McVay III, USN was the commanding officer of the USS Indianapolis}

In 1976, now Dick McVay to me, called and asked that I come to the Indianapolis reunion, which I did. I was informed that I was the only one from the Bassett that had ever called them. When I was introduced to the group, from thereon I was swamped by those who were picked up by the Bassett who wanted to talk with someone from the Bassett. One fellow said he always wanted to meet someone from the

Bassett and find out how they were able to clean up that ship after they left. I told them that I was informed that they cut out all the hammock lashings and burned them. Then they installed all new canvas bunk bottoms. They expressed their deep appreciation of the way the Bassett crew took care of them and what they did to save their lives. It was a very touching experience. Richard C McVay is now deceased.

Another incident concerned a survivor just across from McVays bunk on the Bassett and on the inside bulkhead. He was talking out of his head and rubbing his hands up and down the bulkhead and saying: "Why did they pick us up?" "Why did they pick us up?" "We didn't do anything!" "Why did they pick us up?" I tried to quiet him down and by telling him that he was going to be all right and he would be taken care of. I was dumbfounded on what further to say. It came to mind that when we left the States we had a camouflage paint job on our hull. When we got to Pearl Harbor we went into dry dock and received a battleship grey paint job. When they painted the hull they also painted the four LCVP boats but in doing so the painters covered the boats markings leaving off the "A" in front of the APD so that our boats carried only a PD 73 marking. I was quite sure that this survivor thought the "Police Department " had picked up the survivors and thus his concern.

Also after getting off duty I went to the fantail where the survivors were receiving more medical attention. One of our crew handed me a glass and a wooden spatula with an ointment to touch up the sores on the survivors, when someone said: "I don't believe I've ever seen you before!" It was the Captain of our ship. I informed him I was in the Engineering Division and my station was in the # I Fireroom. He passed on.

/s/James D. Arthur WT3/c
USS Bassett APD 73

63

James S. Bargsley RdM 3/c   December 1998
Crew member USS Bassett

Dear L. Peter Wren:

Received your letter and I think its great that you are putting down in book form experiences of our shipmates and others regarding the rescue of the survivors of the USS Indianapolis. At the time this happened I was making notes and keeping a log. This is how I wrote it in July of 1945.

The most horrible experience I have ever witnessed in the Navy was the night in July 1945. The USS Bassett assigned to the 7th Fleet, was on patrol duty in the Philippine Frontier against Japanese submarines, etc. As a radioman 3rd class I was on watch in the radio shack when an "Urgent" message came in. The communication officer on duty after decoding it rushed it to the Captain for answer and immediate action. The message read that people were sighted in the water on floating rafts dropped by aircraft and for us to proceed with all possible speed to the given latitude and longitude. We were miles away and the sea was rather rough and it took us a while to arrive at the vicinity. It was early the next day about one o'clock am. We had been warned that Japanese subs were in the vicinity, and to be alert. The Captain or the Executive Officer ordered the signal man on watch to keep flashing the signal light in all directions in an on-and-off way looking for floating objects, also so we wouldnt make a good floating target for Jap Subs. After a while a lookout on the bridge spotted a floating object. By coming closer they found it to be debris. Minutes later another object, and going closer we found it to be the body of a floating man. Approximately thirty minutes later the bridge lookout sighted men on a float waving and yelling. Immediately the Captain or the Executive Officer [which I think took over at this time] ordered the LCVP in the water to rescue survivors. Some of this information is hearsay but a

64

lot of it I witnessed when not on watch. My general quarters station was in the emergency radio shack {midships} so if the main radio room was damaged I could send emergency messages out.

At this time we did not know the men were from the USS Indianapolis or what had happened. After a while the LCVP's came back with survivors and some deceased sailors. Some were brought aboard on stretchers or the wire basket [Stokes Stretcher]. Some of the men were out of their minds, yelling and swearing. Most had burns from the sun, with shark bites and were covered with bunker oil.

Our Doctor Royce Pruet aboard the USS Bassett did a great job trying to help these men survive. He was aided by every crew member not on watch. Some did not survive and were put in canvas bags and placed on the fantail of the Bassett for later burial. After two days at sea we arrived at Samar Island in the Philippines with 152 of the 317 that survived the Indianapolis sinking. I am very proud of the USS Bassett's crew and I hope this little information will be helpful.

Sincerely

/s/ James S. Bargsley

P.S.   Enclosed is a picture of the USS Bassett at the Commissioning, Orange, Texas

Ltr from Jack D. Paul   04/26/1998
LCVP #1 Bassett Boat Crew

It was a pitch black night as the USS Bassett approached the area where people earlier in the day had been spotted in the water. Each LCVP [four in all aboard the ship) normally carried a crew of three, consisting of a coxswain, an engineer and a boathook man. On this trip we also carried Officer Ensign Jack Broser of Brooklyn, NY. We pulled away from the Bassett and began to search off the starboard bow. It was very dark and the officer held a battle lantern searching the waters before us. In no time we spotted a group of men holding on to floater nets and a raft of some sort. The men were floating in water thick with black oil. My first thought was that it must have been an oil tanker that had sunk. As we approached the group Ensign Broser drew his 45 pistol and called out for identification as we had no idea who they were. "Indianapolis," someone replied. Not convinced with that answer, he challenged them again with a question about a baseball team. The answer came back correct and we were relieved that they were Americans, not Japanese. There were cries of help and someone was calling for his mother. It was a nightmarish scene. (About 250 of the crew were just out of recruit training).

Our problem now was how to get these sick and injured men into the LCVP without causing further injuries. Most were too weak or injured to climb over the boats high sides even with our help. We tried lowering the boat ramp but the boat was rolling and pitching causing the sea to flow into the well area. It also posed a danger to the survivors of being struck by the pitching ramp, We had to try to pull them up and over the sides and stern which took a tremendous effort on both the survivors and the rescue crew. Finally, having picked up a small number, we decided to return to the Bassett for more help. By now the ship had its deck and search lights turned on so we had no trouble returning to her. That we

66

were a sitting duck for a Japanese torpedo was apparent to all.

We approached the ship's starboard side and got lines aboard to hold the boat steady as we transferred the rescued men to the ships deck. The rolling seas made this task very difficult. When our boat came about even with the Bassetts' deck we would lift and pass a man to waiting hands. It was a dangerous and painful transfer for all hands. (Remember we have the oil from the survivors over everything and footing is precarious) After unloading was completed additional men were ordered into our boat. We then cast off and returned to where the rest of the large group of men were still in the water. [This is where Boats #1 and #2 joined up] One or more of our crew decided to jump into the water to help the survivors get into our boat. This aided the rescue efforts immensely, enabling us to get the injured men into the boat faster and less painful. (Note: Jack Paul doesn't mention the cries of pain or the screams as we try to lift these men over the sides into the boat. He just refers to it as "painful,")

As soon as a boat was filled we headed back to the to the ship. There we were faced with the same problems in transferring men aboard as before. This time however litter baskets were used allowing us to strap in a man and then pass the litter aboard with less danger to all. This was an improvement but was still awkward and exhausting. How many times we shuttled back and forth with survivors and how many our boats rescued I do not know, but we picked up all we saw in that area. The other LCVPs were doing the same thing. Finally the word was passed that the boats were to be brought aboard. The Bassett was getting underway to return to the Philippine Islands where medical units were awaiting our arrival. We were all very tired. The heavy black oil was on everything making it hard to move around in the boat but all boats were lifted aboard without incident. After securing the boats I walked through the passage ways where, instead of troops, sick and injured Indianapolis survivors were being attended to by our crew. I thanked God for guiding us to the rescue area.

/s/ Jack D. Paul

LCVP (Landing Craft, Vehicle & Personnel)
a.k.a. Higgins boats

Earle Houghtaling   April 1998
Bassett crew member

Dear Peter:
        We were at GQ when the first boatload of survivors
arrived along side of the Bassett. I was excused from my gun
position and told to give a hand on the main deck as the
survivors were brought aboard. The first survivor I helped
was Harold J. Bray, Jr who was the first survivor aboard. We
laid the men on the deck as they could not stand. We used
our combat knives to cut the life jacket and their clothes off.
With the thick bunker fuel oil there was no way we could
untie the knots or unbutton shirts. We carefully searched their
pockets and put the contents in a box for them to claim later.
Two Bassett crew members would assist a survivor to the
bunks on each side of the main deck of the ship. These canvas
bunks were set up to accommodate the UDT teams or the
marine landing force we were destined to carry as part of an
invasion force.
        Luckily we did not have the UDT or an invasion force
on board so we really had ample space for the survivors. Only
an APD would be so equipped with these extra bunks, so it
was a blessing we could be an early ship to accomplish the
rescue. Destroyers and destroyer escorts would have to take
the men below and use the crew's facilities. We recovered
152 of the survivors and some did get assigned bunks in the
lower areas and in the Chief Petty Officer areas. I believe we
had 125 bunks that were not in use. We had a regular crew of
190-200 men when all bunks were used. We had at that time
15 Officers aboard with Ensigns Hager and Smook being
recently added. When all the bunks were used I would be
cooking and feeding for 325 men. Being a first class cook in
charge of the watch I had to know how much food to break
out to feed that number of men.

After helping to unload several LCVP's of survivors I was directed by the supply officer, Ensign Russell Lindsey, to get cleaned up and to take charge of the galley. I was also directed to check with Dr Royce Pruet to see what kind of food I should prepare for the survivors. We were fortunate to have just taken on stores before leaving Leyte and had a supply of fresh oranges. We cut the oranges into wedges and took them to the survivors who were lying in the bunks. We pressed the orange slices over their teeth or against their lips and they would open their eyes and try to extract every ounce of juice from the wedges. The ones who didn't respond we left to the doctor and the pharmacist mates as they were dealing with IV solutions. Anyone coming off watch or standing around waiting to help was handed the IV bag and told to hold it until it was empty and then to call the doctor.

After that the doctor said we could give them something more nourishing. We made some tomato soup and served it warm but they seemed to prefer the clearer and cooler liquids like water and juice. Can't recall how long it took but some men made it out of their bunks and came through the chow line. We never did shut down the chow line because the crew was so busy helping they would eat on the run and stand their watch and come right back to help the survivors. For example, it took three men to get the bunker fuel oil off of them. Two to hold the survivor up because the shower floor (deck) was awash in the heavy oil. Then one would take the diesel oil we were using to cut the oil and wash them carefully, paying attention to salt water ulcers, chafing from the life jackets, and possible wounds from shrapnel or burns from the hot decks. Many tried not to cry out as the diesel did its job, some just screamed and others just grunted in pain. When we got the biggest percent of bunker oil off we then applied soap and water to get them clean. Again we had to go around the salt water ulcers, the wounds. and the chafed areas on the legs and under the arms.

70

It was amazing how anxious they were to be rid of that bunker fuel oil and how much they would grimace and bear with us as we labored to clean them. Having that oil on hands and face meant they still were ingesting it and retching and vomiting This is not an easy experience if it continues. They wanted to be free of it so they could eat and drink without "that" taste.

/s/ Earle Houghtaling

Ltr to Ed Kizer from Gunnar G. Gunheim
copy to L. Peter Wren   Nov 13 1997

In late July 1945 while patrolling in the Philippines Sea, we received a cryptic message. We were ordered to proceed with all haste to a designated location to pick up survivors. I recall we traveled at flank speed for many hours. We had not been told what we would find. I was a Sonarman just out of my teens and was on duty in the Sonar hut just below the flying bridge when we arrived at the location after midnight. When we stopped dead in the water I stopped echo ranging and converted to scanning since we did not want to disclose our position to enemy submarines when we were not in a position to attack. The Officer of the Deck turned on the flood lights to scan the water so with permission I secured the sonar gear since we were stopped. The sight was one of horror. I imagined it to be a scene from hell. The sea was alive with moaning figures and we knew not who they were. We unloaded an LCVP manned by a boat officer, an Ensign from New York and his crew. (This was Boat #1 with Ensign Jack Broser in charge) Not knowing who was in the water, we were wary of Japanese tricks and therefore before anyone was rescued we needed to know if they were friendly or foe. Broser, to ascertain who was in the water called out, "In what

71

city do the Dodgers play baseball?" The answer came back "Brooklyn!" Broser cried out, "They are Americans!" and the rescue began in earnest. Survivors were scooped into the LCVP and brought to the fantail (stern of the Bassett) and then brought on board. (Gunnar says the survivors were scooped up but read Jack Paul's and VanWilpe's letters for what actually occurred in boat # 1. In boat #2 Ensign Wren, being taller than Broser, was able to reach over the side of his boat and lift the survivors into his boat)

Gunnar continues--I was still in my hut below the flying bridge when I heard a seaman lookout yell, "Look at that fish!" One of the officers mistook the exclamation to be a torpedo and completely lost his cool. {Gene Bell stated on the telephone to the author that he was on the number one throttle in the fireroom #1 and received an order on the engine order telegraph for "All ahead Full!". Before he could get the throttle all the way open, the order was cancelled.} Ensign Smook, newly commissioned and new on board, heard a loud discussion among the senior officers. Smook was out on the starboard wing of the flying bridge and didn't know what to make of this noisy confusion. Ltjg Anderson [Chief Engineer} had come up on the bridge from the engine room to get the latest information and he told the author that he heard the loud conversations and thought it best to return to his engine spaces. Gunnar's letter continues--that the officer screamed, "Get the LCVP's aboard and let's get the hell out of here!" Another officer in a calm and commanding voice said; "No way--we 're going to stay here until we get every survivor aboard." And we did.

I received permission to leave the bridge and went immediately to the fantail to help where I could. We had one doctor on board and two corpsmen and the rest of us became helpers. We immediately strung hammocks in the passage ways and it became an emergency hospital ship.

Amazingly, some of the survivors after some five days floating in the water came aboard and walked into the mess hall and grabbed themselves a cup of Joe as if they had just gotten off watch. {This could have been the group that was able to get into the life raft dropped by the B-17 which would have contained fresh water and "C" rations} However, the majority were far less fortunate. Those who were clearly dead we laid out on the deck to the rear of the ship. The rest we gently carried to a hammock while the doctor checked each one out. To many he applied IV bottles or other medications and we then began the task of cleaning off the stinking black oil that clung to everyone. Even though this was some 50 years ago I recall the stench of oily death most vividly.

The LCVP boat crews continued to feed us boatload after boatload of survivors. The sea was now restless and rolling with ten foot swells not uncommon. I recall a LCVP approaching us nearly rolling over and spilling three exhausted survivors back into the sea, apparently to their death. Suddenly a figure from the crew of the LCVP jumped into the sea, and surfaced with not one-- not two-but all three survivors grasped in his arms. They all survived. The hero turned out to be a Gunners mate striker who was a large ungainly quiet farm boy to whom I had never spoken. When he came back aboard I clasped his hand and praised him warmly for what I had witnessed. Another of his crew mates said, "You should have seen him out there--he did the same thing two other times!" [This was William VanWilpe gunners mate striker.]

Although we had been awake and busy for many hours none of our crew hit the sack. We waited on the bed ridden like cats on a new born kitten. I recall one asking me for water. I scurried to fetch a cup of cold water. "This is too cold," he said.

We searched the seas, by now it was light, and we were satisfied that there were no more to be saved. We proceeded under flank speed to a hospital station in the Philippines and gently unloaded our precious survivors. To a man, the coherent of the survivors, were appreciative and grateful to us and we basked in the adulation and became more decent human beings because of it. We had been preparing for the invasion of Japan, but several days later the atomic bomb was dropped and soon thereafter the Japanese surrendered.

Gunheim, adds a third page to his original letter and continues. As we approached the approximate search area, Radarman 3/c Bob Pettitt (in CIC) thought he saw something on the radar screen and alerted the Ensign Watch Officer. The Ensign looking carefully at the radar screen concluded, "Aw, those are just fog clouds on the water, forget about them." However the 1st class Radarman on watch questioned the Ensign's decision and invited the Captain to check out the findings. The Captain said:" They may well be clouds but we better take a look." Thank God we did!

The LCVP leading boat men that night were George Leigh, Jack Paul and Earl Knight according to Gunnar Gunheim and were the heroes that controlled the boats so that the survivors could be brought aboard. [The author concurs on their skillful handling.]

/s/ Gunnar Gunheim

Telephone call from George Leigh.   December 1998
USS Bassett crew

George Leigh was a boat crewman on LCVP #1 with
Ensign Jack Broser during the night of the rescue. He doesn`t
recall how many trips they made that night to rescue the
Indianapolis survivors. He does remember when he was
finally released from rescue duty, he made his way aft and
below toward the enlisted men's berthing. To his surprise
when he arrived at his bunk he found it occupied, so again he
called on his reserve strength and scrambled up the ladder to
the main and then to the boat deck. Walking forward to the
LCVP nesting area he found open space on the deck and
collapsed into sound slumber, sans pillow, sans blanket, sans
bunk.

In speaking about his night's experience he states that
he never learned who bumped him out of his bunk. He felt it
was a survivor who was brought below and he was glad to
offer his bunk for someone in greater need. Upon awakening
his mind raced with these words: "If someone had just
lowered a boat the men could have faired better on that
tumultuous sea." With this thought playing over on his mind,
he wrote this little verse.

LOWER AWAY

The sea was high, the night was dark
The men were dying from the bite of the shark

A ship had gone down and the men were afloat
Many were dying for the want of a boat.

A thousand or so souls were lost that day
For the want of the order to "Lower Away!
                    George Leigh August 1945

Earl Knight Metalsmith 1/c   Fall 1998
Bassett Crew

      As we were patrolling off Leyte Island of the
Philippine Islands in later July 1945, we received a message in
the afternoon to proceed to check our survivors in the water.
After dark we went to Battle Stations as we came upon the
survivors. I was in the first LCVP boat over the side, of
which we had four on board. Going out into the blackness we
arrived at some nets and I called out for an American name.
The survivors were clinging to the nets covered with black
gummy fuel oil and you could not recognize them. Back came
the reply--USS Indianapolis-a heavy cruiser. Working swiftly.
we loaded the boat with the survivors and took off for the
ship.
      That night was awesome. A gruesome reality of the
war came home to me. We had to jump into the shark
infested waters and cut the life belts loose where buddies
were belted together and clinging to the nets. Many did not
believe they were being rescued and we had to yell in their
ears and pull them to make them let go of the net. Many had
burns, shark bites, sunburn and salt water sores and would
cry out in agony when you touched them. Feeling
compassion, but with a sense of urgency you had to continue
loading them. Load after load we took back to the ship. We
had to put many of them on stretchers and pull them over the
side of the ship onto the deck to waiting hands. They were so
weak that they could not stand up. The boats worked all
night and near dawn we had 152 rescued sailors. Other ships
came near dawn and we left the scene to take our rescued
sailors to the nearest hospital on Samar Island. Working
tirelessly our ship's doctor cared for the burned and wounded
men. Some had shark bites you could put your hand into.
What a fantastic job the doctor (and crew) did trying to take

care of all 152 men. He told us (the ships crew) to cut little slices of oranges and let the thirst-crazed men suck on them.

We lost one man from shock. I was passing the doctor in the bunking compartment while the doctor was checking on one of the survivors. He gave the man an IV bottle in his arm and handed it to me as he moved on. The sailor in the bunk asked if he was on a hospital ship and I said: "No, you're on an APD!" He asked if I was a corpsman and I said, 'No, I'm a metalsmith 1st class." He asked how come I was holding the IV and I said, "The doctor told me to hold it!"

The whole crew worked tirelessly holding up the weakened men while others scrubbed off the [bunker] fuel oil. Then they were washed down with soap and water, and finally some clean Skivvies [tee shirt & shorts] were put on them. The ship's decks and bulkheads were covered with black slimy bunker fuel oil. Many unsung heroes were made that night, helping these men.

/s/ Earl Knight

Bray's Body Parts

Ltr from Earle Houghtaling SC 1/c   Winter 1997

The first man helped aboard the USS Bassett from the group of survivors of the Indianapolis was Harold J Bray, a seaman 2nd class. The mate that helped Bray was Ship's cook first class Earle Houghtaling who had very carefully cut his oil soaked clothing from his body in preparation for his shower. Earle said he had to be careful with the combat knife he was using because the blade was very sharp and some times the survivor would roll or pitch his body to a different angle. Earle didn't want to be the cause of any more suffering by a misguided blade. After fifty some years the two men were going to meet at Brays home for their first time since that night aboard the ship. After a long and pleasant meeting and introduction to his lovely wife and his handsome family of several boys and girls, Earle said, "Seeing the size of your family, it appears I did no harm when I cut your oily clothes off fifty years ago." Glancing at each other the family agreed it was nice to have such a good-size family, and there was no apparent harm rendered to father Bray's body that evening 50 some years ago.

/s/ Earle Houghtaling
SC 1/c

Ltr #1 from William VanWilpe
Crew member USS Bassett   20 March 1999

Dear Mr Wren

When I saw you on TV and heard your voice I was really surprised. Your story of Ensign Broser's asking the survivors about the Brooklyn Dodgers was true. It was at dusk on the night of August 2, 1945 when we went to [GQ] general quarters. When on my GQ station in the 5"38 gun mount, I put on the head telephones and was directed to get several pairs of binoculars. I was to take a couple of the gun mount men with me and go to the bow of the ship. The three of us would serve as lookouts for survivors. I was the shell man in the 5" mount, so I took my powder man, Buddy Burkett of Atmore, Alabama, and the gun captain, Ken Beale, a gunner's mate 3/c, from Montana. We went up to the anchors. I took the port side with Buddy on the starboard side and Kenny Beale was in the center of the bow by the jack staff.

It was not long before I spotted movement in my search area. I reported my findings to the Officer of the Deck's telephone talker and then asked Buddy and Kenny also to search my area. In no time reports were coming from lookouts all over the ship. The order was then given to put the LCVP's in the water. (This is about 12:40 am)

It did not take long to get the word the survivors were from the USS Indianapolis. Then over the telephone I heard our crew was having trouble getting the survivors aboard. The ship's crew had to coordinate with the LCVP crews to catch the high wave which brought the LCVPs up to about the level of the ship's deck so they could easily transfer the survivors. The waves were cresting between six to ten feet along side of the ship. The survivors of shorter stature were at a greater disadvantage. Being one of the taller Bassett crew members I asked to be relieved from my bow

79

duties so I could be more helpful where the transferring was being done. It was plain to see that the most help needed was in the LCVPs, so I went over the side and into the LCVPs to help.

The first few survivor transfers to the Bassett were accomplished rather easily. The procedure was to lift the survivor up on the right shoulder and at the right timing with the waves, I would use my right arm to push the survivor to the waiting hands on the Bassett. Several other men of our crew were doing the same thing but then things changed. We had a good wave but before I could push a survivor up on my right shoulder the LCVP dropped out from under my feet and the man on my shoulder began to fall. I reached up to grab him, and he landed upon both my shoulders. I couldn't help the man because somehow my right arm separated from my shoulder. There was a gap where my arm and shoulder met. My right arm just dangled at my right side. I turned my body to try to get some help. I heard a popping sound and the right arm was back in place. Most of the pain was gone. It was like nothing had ever happened.

After all these years since the rescue of the survivors, I still have vivid recollections of helping to get the men aboard. Any movement above my right shoulder as I pursue work, hobby or a game reminds me not to tempt fate around this shoulder. Good luck with the book from an old shipmate.

Sincerely

/s/ Bill VanWilpe

                    The Conga. Line
Dear Peter:

We shoved off from the side of the USS Bassett and it didn't take long for the coxswain to have us in an area where the survivors were waiting for rescue. I could see why it took so long to pick up the survivors. Half of the boat crew was holding on to the legs of other boat crewmen spread eagle on the fantail of the LCVP boat. There is no guard rail to hang on to so crewman "A" must hold the crewman "B" from falling overboard as crewman "B" tries to pull a survivor over the fantail of the LCVP, and into the boat. Ensign Broser is short and cannot reach the survivors floating off the side of his LCVP, so they try to bring the survivors over the stern end of the boat which is the part nearest the water.

The survivors would reach up to grasp the hands of boatman "B" on the fantail of the LCVP. Several times the survivor would fall back into the water. After five days in the water the survivors were very weak and lacked their strong arms to pull themselves up about three feet. With boatman "B" prone on the deck of the LCVP he had very little leverage past his shoulder height. Seaman "A" would hold the legs of seaman "B" as he tried to lift the survivor from the water. In my first letter I told you about my right shoulder. I felt I couldn't depend on it so I jumped over the side of the LCVP rather than dive into the water to help get the survivors aboard.

When Ensign Broser saw me in the water he went wild. I had a group of five or six men and I led them to the stern of the LCVP. Using the same technique as we had used at the Bassett, I would get under the rump of the survivor with my shoulders. Then I would rise as high as I could until someone in the LCVP grabbed the survivor. When I swam off to gather some more of the survivors, Ensign Broser again ordered me to get aboard. I told him if he would join me we could get the survivors loaded much easier. He must have thought this was a better method, because he dove over the port side to help out. We were no longer using the men as spread eagles with another mate holding them down on the fantail of the LCVP. Loading from both sides was sure speeding things up.

Many of the men were hallucinating and not very cooperative. I am sure Ensign Broser soon found out that the survivors would not trust him. You would have to lie to the survivors, and the bigger the lie, the better the results. I told them I was going to a "ferry boat" and after they thought about it they followed me. I also got some results by having the men form a "conga line" where we were going to dance. However some things never change. I had a good size group and I had them look at the LCVP which I called the "liberty launch" and we were all going on shore leave. To some nothing worked. You would have to overpower them so they would go with you. I had a group going to the stern of the LCVP when Ensign Broser told me to get aboard. There was no room for more survivors because the LCVP was fully loaded. Had we added more, the ones standing would be trampling those lying down.

If I thought Ensign Broser was wild when I went over the side earlier, it was nothing compared to when I told him I was going to stay with the survivors. After Ensign Broser accepted my decision, the LCVP pulled away slowly from my latest herd so that he wouldn't throw too much wake up on them. I stayed with the survivors because they were disappointed. They were so close to rescue and now they were not sure what was going to happen.

I was really happy to see the LCVP return even though I was throwing up the salt water which was highly flavored with the bunker fuel oil. The wretching really sapped my strength. On my way back to the Bassett, I started to wonder how we could do this better. Some times I would get a survivor and he would fight or he would yell he was going below for water, food, or whatever was on his mind. One man wanted to go below to write a letter home. The men would go under so quickly. I would go down three to five feet and if I did not surface in a hurry the group would scatter. It would take more time to round them up. I was only out there a short time and I was really sick. I wondered how the men survived wallowing in that sickening salt water day after day. They were something special.

Your shipmate

/s/ Bill VanWilpe

LCVP (Landing Craft, Vehicle & Personnel)
a.k.a. Higgins boats

Away Boat – Two

Ensign L. Peter Wren USNR
Night of August 3rd 1945

After my LCVP was water borne and heading on the course directed by CIC (Combat Info Center) we came upon a very large group of men, perhaps 75-100, of an unknown nationality. With a battle lantern I am looking at a black face, white teeth, round white eyed men with black curly hair floating together in the water. Mind you, all they can see is a round white light shining on them and hear a motor running. No one speaks so I call out, "Who are you and what ship are you from?" Back came words used only in the slang of an American Sailor; "Just like a --- --dumb Officer, always asking ------dumb ass questions!" There was no doubt in my mind that they were American sailors. When queried as to what ship were they were from---there was no answer. Then comes more sailor lingo, "Shove off you dumb bastard, who needs your------help!" Hey these guys still have fight and are not quite sure if I'm a friend or a foe. I directed the coxswain to come about to the lee side of the blackened mass and we would start to pick them up. There are too many for my boat so I must get help. I tried to reach Ltjg Ralph Horwitz in CIC requesting Jack Broser's boat come quickly to my scene since there were more people in the water than I could handle. I could only get Ralph on the FCR (short wave radio gear) when I was on the top of a wave. When in the gully between waves there was no communication. My boathook man continued to hold the light on the group in the water while I wrestled with the communication problem with Ralph. At last the message was completed and I understood Broser's boat was on the way to my location.

Some of the survivors thought I was a Jap coming to capture them. Others who were rational wanted to know if I had any water on board. Off to the right was a mate telling others that the Scuttle Butt was two decks down and that the water was cool and very good. He then surfaced dived and disappeared below. I can't recall his resurface so I don't know whether he ever appeared again. The sea is rough and the waves are about six to eight feet between the gully and the crest. The coxswain does a great job getting up close to them and as a high wave brings a survivor close to me, I lean over the gunwale and grab him under the arms. His weight is a combination of a 150 pound man and a water soaked life jacket of equal weight. So I am trying to lift about 300 pounds over the gunwale on a moving and bobbing craft. This man lets out a scream of agony that would pierce a mother's heart. I feel like I am pulling his flesh and muscle away from the bone. I let go and quickly grab on to the life jacket and continue to lift him while waiting for the next wave to assist me.

My boathook man is a lad of 18-19 and is handling the battle lantern so I can see what I'm doing. The other member of our crew is the coxswain who is trying to get me into position to pick up the next survivor by carefully maneuvering the boat. My next survivor, who I have a good hold on his life jacket, decides, I am a Jap trying to capture him and he commences to flail his arms at my head.

When we approached the water borne people we had our 45 caliber pistols drawn with the safety catch unlocked. We didn't know what we would find. So now when you read about Jack Broser's challenge to those in the water you will have a better understanding of what is taking place. Broser is from Brooklyn, New York and his world revolved around the Dodgers and Leo "the lip" Durocher. By this time Broser's boat is arriving on the scene and Jack not knowing what he's looking at, cuts his engines and calls out, "What city do the Dodgers play baseball in?" The answer comes back with a clear call of "Brooklyn." With that Jack puts his boat in an

85

equal position to mine with the men in the water between us. At this moment someone gives the call of "Japs" and one of the survivors takes off from the group as to get away. Jack Broser doffs his hat, and gun belt and dives over the side of his LCVP in hot pursuit of the wayward swimmer. Jack overtakes him and hauls him back to the rest of the group. With this maneuver it seems that the survivors realized we were there to rescue them. Their prayers were being answered. Jack's swimming rescue in this open sea with the six to eight foot waves is a very heroic act and should have been recognized. They move toward the LCVP's and were more helpful in getting aboard. However some were not ready to sit in the boat as they wandered around looking for water. My only answer to that was: "I'd get it in a minute." At this time I still didn't know what ship they were from. I didn't leave the scene until I had a full boat load. A boat load would consist of about six sitting on the deck of the boat, three or four lying flat on the deck and two to three wandering around where I am standing looking for water. Before I left I called over to Jack to stay with the men until I could get back. I didn't want them to feel we were abandoning those not yet picked up. I didn't know who had command of the third boat or where it was.

When I turned my attention away from the men I looked to the rear of the LCVP hoping to see the lights of our ship. It was an absolutely pitch black night and there wasn't a star or a glimmer of light anywhere. I turned on the FCR hand held radio and ask Ltjg Horwitz to turn on a search light so I would have a beacon to the Bassett. There is no way I could return on a reciprocal course from which I arrived on the scene as the wind and sea had carried us wherever it pleased. I was not going to get lost on the Philippine Sea with a group of men needing attention. I have read other books on the evening of the rescue and all seem to indicate that all the ships lights were lit. However I do see 20/20 and I tell you I was there and there was no lights on my first load of survivors until someone on the bridge turned the lights on. Further from my view, between the six and eight foot waves, it was the blackest overcast night I have ever encountered.

When we got along side of the Bassett, they had a Jacobs ladder over the port side rear quarter of the ship. Unloading the survivors from the LCVP was very difficult even though we were in the lee of the sea as provided by the ship. Some of the survivors with the help of those on the deck and a steady push from us in the LCVP made it to the deck of the Bassett. Some were so weak that they could not stand up in the rolling LCVP so I called for the Stokes stretcher (wire basket) to get them aboard. On my second load of survivors I picked up Ensign Blum who was able to climb the ladder rather quickly and was escorted to see our Captain. The rest of the men who couldn't climb the Jacobs ladder, lacking the strength, were aided by Bassett crew members who came down into the LCVP's to assist them. Between the men pushing from the LCVPs and the pulling from the men on the deck of the Bassett we got them aboard. Once unloaded we shoved off again for another load of survivors. And so we continue through the night. The number of LCVP loads I made that night I am not sure.

On about the fourth or fifth load of survivors one of my shipmates offered me a cup of coffee and I gladly climbed up on the deck of the Bassett to take advantage of his offer. It was then when I tried a sip of the hot cup of coffee that the fuel oil all over me on my face and hands made the cup of nice smelling coffee taste like what I was wearing. I stepped near our submarine depth charges to pitch the cup over the side when I noticed someone coming down on our afterdeck in a boatswains chair carrying a black bag. The other end of the line was coming out of the hawse pipe of the USS Madison DD425. The skipper of that ship had put the bow of his destroyer over our starboard quarter. Man, what a feat of seamanship on that rough sea. The boatswain chair's occupant was Doctor Harlan A. Stiles coming to aid our Doctor Royce Pruet. (I read in one book that an LCVP was sent to pick him up.) However that was not my observation as all the Bassett boats were involved with the rescue mission.

On another occasion I climbed up on the deck of the Bassett so shipmates could go down into LCVPs slippery oiled deck to help boost the survivors up the Jacobs ladder. On this occasion a motor whaleboat was tied up on the starboard side of the quarterdeck. A shipmate was arguing with a survivor in the whaleboat to the effect that the survivor would not leave the whaleboat until we came down into the whaleboat and helped his "buddy" aboard. The "buddy" was slumped over the engine housing, and not responding to either of the two arguing. It was then I yelled at the survivor in the whaleboat to "Knock it off and get up on the deck of the Bassett!" The survivor did as I had directed and I believed the man slumped over the engine housing had died. [In fact, it was at the 1999 Indy reunion that Richard Stephens approached the Bassett table and stated: "I passed out over the engine housing of the whale- boat the B-17 had dropped!" After 54 years, I got to meet this survivor personally.]

At this moment I was feeling great fatigue and it was when Petty Officer L. F. Shay MM2/c, of the engineering gang, offered to relieve me. Reaching over that gunwale and lifting those survivors with all those water soaked life jackets was very difficult and exhausting. The survivors chins were at the water level and there didn't appear to be much floatation left in those jackets. I knew I had to continue to pull them over the gunwale but the offer sounded very practical. I was spent of strength and energy. I accepted gratefully and left the fantail making my way toward my quarters. Shipmates were helping the survivors in the "troop carrying area." The place reeked of fuel oil but the deck was not as slippery as the deck on my LCVP. Getting below to my quarters, I stripped off my oil soaked uniform, down to my oil soaked skivvies and flopped in my sack. Lifting those water and oil soaked men over the gunwale of the LCVP had drained me. Once relieved the adrenalin stopped flowing, and the cries of agony had ceased and I was asleep from exhaustion.

I knew it was a terrible tragedy but not as horrible as it turned out. We had no idea how many were lost. We had no idea how many were recovered by the other ships. Ltjg Horwitz advised later on that by sunrise the sea area was filled with rescue ships. We had no idea of the Indy's mission and how close the Japanese were to surrendering. The boat crew serving with me that night have never been recognized and I'd like to take this moment to thank those two young men still in their "teens" who were called on to do a man's job and they performed heroically. I have never served with better shipmates. I regret I never learned their names as we rotated training with different crews depending what watch section was on duty. The boat officers were assigned to a specific boat and when that boat was called he accepted whatever crew had the duty.

Although more than fifty years have passed I can still see our crew of young faces laboring with the task before them. I can still see those oil blackened faces in the sea and I can hear their cries of agony. When we sing the Navy Hymn I still well up when we come to the last line "For those in Peril on the sea." It will never leave me!

/s/ L. Peter Wren

Recollections by Jack D. Paul
October 6 and 7, 1945
Aboard the USS Bassett

Kure Naval Base, Honshu, Japan

     The USS Bassett was loaded with a contingent of US Army troops to be transported to Kure, Japan for the purpose of placing American Occupational troops at their large Kure Naval Base. Kure, Japan is located on the Inland Sea on the large Island of Honshu and just south of the atom bombed city of Hiroshima.

     The American troops prior to boarding the Bassett were veterans of Pacific campaigns and were to be rotated states side when they received new orders directing them to this new assignment. Naturally they were not thrilled with this situation, but, coming aboard the USS Bassett offered more amenities than they had seen since they left the United States. First there were showers with fresh hot water. Second there were no fox holes to be dug, and third there were three prepared meals every day on a regular schedule, with coffee pots brewing fresh "Joe" for these G.I. Joes. Snacks were also available and desserts with every meal. No need to eat those dried rations or boil anything in you helmet. Powdered milk fresh from a chilled refrigeration system plus powdered eggs every morning was like eating in a first class French restaurant. They concluded the Navy knew how to fight a war. Thank God for the calm waters of the Inland Sea because there was no sea sickness as we plowed the waters between the homeland islands of Honsho, and Shikoku. Every Army man had his own clean bunk and there were no K.P. [Kitchen Police] details for our US Army guests.

     We left Wakayama, Japan on 4 October and sailed for the Kure Naval Base about 330 miles away. Upon arrival we dropped anchor among other US Naval vessels and awaited instructions as to when we would move our Army guests to their new location. The USS Bassett is designated as a "Fast Troop Transport" and has the four LCVPs aboard for putting an armed force ashore quickly. We observed a Japanese launch leaving their Naval base and heading for one of the large USS vessels also swinging on the hook[anchored]. The Japanese dignitaries disappeared aboard the American ship and we presumed that the arrangements were being made as to the US Army take over.

Watching from the bridge of our ship, on the long glass [large binoculars] we saw the Japanese Delegation reappear and their launch headed back to their Naval Base. The Bassett's boat crews were now along side and loading our Army guests for a landing on the shores of the Japanese Naval Base. As the LCVPs made their way toward the beach there was concern and apprehension that perhaps some of the militant and die hard Japanese would try something to disrupt the occupation. Our LCVP crews ran the vessels up on the beach and lowered the ramps. The Army personnel disembarked and formed up on the Naval Base awaiting further orders. There appeared to be no problems so the LCVPs were ordered back to the USS Bassett.

From the bridge the Bassett crew watched the Japanese lower their War Flag, fold it up and march off to one side of the field. The US Army contingent then proceeded to raise the American Flag on the same pole which was then followed by all the American troops saluting it. Then the Japanese senior officer came forward, bowed and presented his sword. The US Army senior officer accepted it, thanked the officer, and then handed it right back to him. Having witnessed our first occupational event we were pleased with our helping to secure the peace we all welcomed.

Hiroshima

Phone call from Vernon S. Skordahl
crew member USS Bassett   April 1999

When the USS Bassett finished escorting the group of LCMs to the area of Kure, Japan the ship was very close to the area of the Hiroshima bombing. Skordahl was assigned to a Shore Patrol team to escort Japanese truck drivers to a specific warehouse in the area of the LCVP landing docks. Skordahl said it was like in the "Old West Movies" in that the shore patrol was riding escort (shot gun) with their Japanese drivers to make sure they went to the correct warehouse. The cargo was a very large amount of Japanese rifles and swords which were being put under United States control.

When the shore party arrived at the assignment area they noted that they were on the edge of where the Hiroshima bomb was dropped. The Japanese civilian workers were all wearing cloth face masks which covered their nose and mouth. The shore patrol did not receive any type of cloth mask and became concerned. The ground was covered with a grey white powder which as one walked about in it became an air borne dust which they were inhaling. Their shoes and leggings were beginning to collect the grey powder. No effort was made to provide the shore patrol with protective masks.

Looking in toward the center of the area, Skordahl said there seem to be a saucer like depression that was full of rubble. The foundations of building and homes were slightly visible. He said you could see a few railings and steps leading up to a building. The area was very flat and the grey white dust seemed to be everywhere. There weren't any land marks so it was hard to judge distance. He thought the center was about 5 to 6 miles away. It could have been more.

They mounted the loaded trucks with the Japanese drivers and with the maps provided, directed the drivers by sign language to the landing dock warehouses. After several trips on the trucks, Skordahl and his shore patrol buddies were getting bored with the same dirty road and flat area. Since the drivers knew the route to the warehouses they put them under their own cognizance and let them make the trips on their own. They walked around the area but there wasn't much to see so they proceeded to the meeting area for transport back to the LCVP docks.

The next day Skordahl drew the shore patrol assignment again and after a short meeting with his group, they sent the drivers on their rounds without escort. The shore patrol did not receive face masks on the second day and were concerned about their exposure to the radiation from the atomic bombing. With no protection provided and since the Japanese drivers were performing what was expected of then without escort, the shore patrol group took a short tour of the area and then gathered up a few of the souvenir items for their friends who had the duty aboard the ship.

The Bassett departed the area and put into the harbor of Nagasaki where Skordahl drew a shore patrol assignment again. This time he refused to obey the orders of his division officer. He was given a captain's mast, which is a form of a hearing of the case by the ship's Captain, and with proper punishment meted to the offender of the rules. Skordahl was given 100 hours of extra duty and confined to the ship until it was completed. The boatswain mate was to see that the punishment was carried out and when completed report back to the Captain.

Skordahl is in his seventies and reports he is enjoying good health in spite of his exposure in Hiroshima.

/s/ Vernon Skordahl

Chapter Three

Includes pictures of the USS Bassett and the crew. Maps of the Philippine Sea Area and the location of the various islands that will help the reader understand the story better.

The cover, maps and various drawings are the work of William W. McCathern, Jr. Several shipmates have provided photographs of the men and the USS Bassett. The US Naval Institute is the source of the historic pictures of the ships.

USS BASSETT (APD-73)   (taken in 1951)

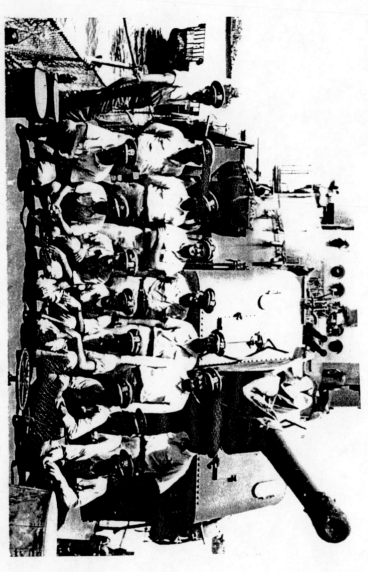

USS BASSETT's officers assembled on the foredeck in Leyte Harbor in late August 1945. L to R, front row: De Lisle, Hager, Smook, Horwitz, Broser, Van Dyke, Lindsey, and Dr. Pruet. Back Row: Leweke, Axtell, Nagle, Theriault, Henderson, Wren, Anderson and Evans.

USS BASSETT's crew assembled on the fantail in Orange, Texas

Ensign L. Peter Wren USNR (the author) - Deck officer on watch, USS BASSETT - Pacific Ocean

Ruins of Manila Police Headquarters

San Luis Church lies in ruin

Chapter Four

Oral histories and letters from
the USS Indianapolis Survivors

Ltr From Harold Bray
March 1998

Dear Sir:

     We left Mare Island on 16 July 1945 with the Bomb on board, but of course we didn't know what was in the box. We delivered this box to Tinian Island in the Marianas and left for Guam on 28 July. Two days later we were hit by torpedoes from a Japanese submarine. The ship sank in twelve minutes. I went over the side of the ship and into the water a little after midnight on 30 July. We found a float net and somehow unrolled it and started to gather survivors. The men that were badly burned or hurt were put on the floaters. When daylight came I think we had about 140-160 men in the group with one life raft and one life net to hang on to and share among us. A floater net is a 20 foot square of rope woven together at each twelve inch intersection with a cork or air foam rubber float secured in the space between the joined rope intersections. The floater net is stored topside in open tubs on all US Navy ships. In case of a sinking it will float free to the ocean surface. The net was our refuge from where the sharks and the sun took their toll..

     Well you know the rest of the story. Airplanes flew over us every day without spotting us. It was very depressing. On the fourth day we were found and the rescue started. Gwinn' s plane dropped what I thought was water. I swam out to it to only discover it was some sort of sub detector. I couldn't get back to the group because I was too tired. Anyway, they were having too much trouble with sharks. Luckily I found a raft with two other survivors and that is where I stayed until the next morning when you and the wonderful Bassett showed up. It was still dark and I could see the big flood light off in the distance. it kept getting closer, finally, the landing craft spotted me. I was alone on the raft. I don't know what happened to the other two sailors that I hooked up with earlier. This landing craft pulled up and someone said, "Hey sailor, can you climb this ladder or rope?" I tried and, of course, I was too weak. I fell back into the water and someone came over the side and got me into the craft. We were transported back to the ship and lifted one by one, as gently as possible onto the deck. I was taken to what I thought was some kind of a hospital room. Doctors or corpsmen examined me and asked if I had any broken bones or wounds. They took what clothes I had on, off and put me into a shower where I passed out. I woke up in a bunk all cleaned up with someone cleaning the oil out of my eyes and ears. The treatment that I received was so good that I thought everyone of your crew was a doctor.

I found out later that most of your crew were sailors like myself. They gave us juice and water, but just enough to get our strength back. The treatment on board that ship was as good as any hospital treatment. I would like to thank you and the rest of the crew of the Bassett for the rescue and the treatment after the rescue.

/s/Harold Bray

Ltr from Donald J. Blum [PE]

Dear Peter:

As you requested I will try my memory to give you some material for your story about what happened to me aboard your ship-the Bassett.

You are aware that when you found our little group about 12, as I recall, we were aboard an inflatable raft dropped to us about 10 hours previously. The raft had been a pilots raft built for two. It was absolutely submerged with us sailors athwartships, one on top of another. We had with us also a single raft or pieces of one that had supported a few of us with life jackets. We were all covered with oil. After I got aboard the raft I fell asleep with someone on top of me. I was awakened by others when they realized rescue was imminent. I woke to see a tremendous headlight shining on us. When your LCVP was downstream from the light I noted someone was aiming a machine gun at us. There was some conversation between our group and yours, but I did not trust it in view of possibly being a target and I slipped into the water. Soon came the realization that we were being rescued and I certainly allowed that to happen.

I remember that the craft took us to the side of the Bassett and to a cargo net. As I recall, I did not waste any time climbing aboard with some help from the crew. I also noted that I probably was one of the very few who could climb aboard and also walk. I was told the Captain wanted to see me but I stopped for a drink at the first fountain and almost drained it dry. My escort for the trip to the bridge seemed somewhat impatient with my drinking and as I started to leave, I shortly returned for some more water. I arrived at the bridge to be introduced to the Captain who was actively conning the ship. I did tell him I had been on the Indianapolis that had been sunk. He was unaware of exactly why he had been sent to the area or how many survivors there might be. He, against standing orders, turned on all the lights so as not to run down others still in the water. As far as I know, your ship was the only one to break the rules and used your radio to request doctors and to light up so as to rescue as many as possible. From my vantage on the bridge, I could tell that no other ship displayed lights.

You are aware of the tomato soup versus the tomato juice story as it has been published. I think I startled the person who brought it to me, but it was very hot in that climate and I had really thought cold juice would be nice. I had partially slaked my thirst by then. Later, I wandered from the bridge to where my former shipmates were being ministered. They were on troop canvas cots and most were comatose. I noted that the doctors had ordered them to be fed about one quarter cup of water every half hour and they were dissatisfied with that. I would have been. Thank goodness that I got aboard before the doctors and I had as much water as I could hold at that time. Your crew was also handing out orange slices I think. After I saw that things were progressing and there was little I could do, I decided it was time to find a more comfortable spot to sleep. At some point, I remember that the Bassett would be cutting out of the operation because there were several other ships now in the area and that there was a full load of rescued now on board. The other ships would stick around to give further help. It was also indicated that several survivors needed hospital care and that was not possible aboard.

I found the troop officers quarters with some nice thick mattresses and flaked out. I arose sometime the next morning, black as the ace of spades, and started out of the compartment to find food and water. I wandered by the Chiefs quarters and they invited me in to have a cup of coffee. They said that breakfast was over and my best bet was to sit and partake of what they had there. They also suggested that I wash with some kerosene and also supplied me with a pair of shorts. I had abandoned my clothes before I went to bed because they were completely oil soaked. After washing as best possible, I got a cup of coffee. Canned milk was not offered, only some sugar. One swig of the coffee convinced me that it contained some alcohol, and that was not all bad. As I remember a few minutes later I returned to my bunk room for a rest. I had noticed though that the bunk I had slept on before had oil stains on the underside. I took another bunk. I woke up again about lunch time and made my way to the wardroom for lunch.

On my way to the lunch, I noted everything I touched turned black. Apparently the oil was still coming off me. I forget what transpired at lunch except that talk was of the rescue operation. I noted the Captain said he hoped that the rescued would not mess up the boat too much and that we should be careful what we touched. He told someone that the survivors should not use the troop officers quarters because mattresses were hard to clean. I did not volunteer any information on that subject. I had already ruined two and I saw others in a similar condition.

As I recall, we were told that we would be taken to Samar in the Philippines. This took a couple of days. We arrived there, I in my oil-stained shorts, to be taken to a hospital where we were held incommunicado for a week while the Navy was trying to figure out how to break the news of the tragedy. Ultimately the sinking was announced on V-J day [August 15, 1945]. The notice made only a little dent in the front page of the New York Times. It appeared in a few other papers at that time as well.

I hope the above helps you with your story. Why should I not help? You rescued me. Of course in the Chinese custom you are now responsible for me and I appreciate that.

Very truly yours,
/s/ Donald J. Blum
fmr Ensign USNR

Ltr from Sherman C. Booth   Summer 1998
Indy Survivor

Dear Peter:

All that I remember is that sometime after about 0100 am on the third I was picked up. I don't remember seeing the ships coming because at that time there were many sailors in our group that were hallucinating. I began to ignore them as though nothing was happening. Until I was being picked up out of the water I thought I was imagining things myself. When I realized this was for real I remembered everything except who unfastened me from the rest of the group. I was fastened good so that I would not drift away.

You took me aboard on the port side near the fantail. You had to use a stretcher to haul me aboard. The first thing I had was a cup of soup which was delicious. I drank it in one gulp. I didn't know until the next morning that it was boiling hot when I complained of having a sore throat. As soon as they saw what had happened I heard someone say, "Don't give them any more hot soup!" You were trying to do what you thought was best for us. Nothing like this had ever happened before and everyone had to guess what to do (even the doctors). I never was so tired and hungry and sleepy in my life and I think you knew that. I remember you cleaned us with oil, grease and lard, and I thought I heard one say that he had some butter and that might help to get the oil off us. One mate kept laughing at my chest; about the match sticks

101

that were matted in my hair which were about 2 to 2 1/2 inches long. I don't know where they came from or how they got there. [Note: some life jackets have little metal tubes of matches attached which are needed to start a fire or light signal flares.]

I never had so much kind and considerate care as I got from the ones who took care of me. (Thank you). I do remember they cleaned the oil until our hides started to slip (which had no feeling), then they would switch to some kind of soap. I slept through most of that. They had us lying on the deck in the shower while they cleaned. All they had to do was to roll us until we were clean.

After I was put in bed I felt so good that all I wanted to do was to sleep, but they knew that food and liquids were more important. So every time one of us would move, someone would be there to ask if we needed something, or was there something they could do for us. They treated us like kings. I have to tell you this before what I tell will make any sense.

As you well know, when you are taking on supplies and you got a chance, you would take some of the food stuff and store it, in case the kitchen [galley] fed something you couldn't eat. My storage was spam and cheese. We could always get a loaf of bread from the ships baker. We could help ourselves to the onions always stored above the main deck and not locked. So when we broke out our stores we had spam, cheese and onion sandwiches. I thought of that constantly. When I went to sleep I would dream of these sandwiches and I would wake up to see if these sandwiches were real or if I was hallucinating.

Anyway when they had us cleaned up and in bed, someone came up and asked if I wanted anything at all. If they didn't have it they would try to get it for me. My request was that I wanted a "spam and cheese" sandwich. He was quick to return with it and when I tried to take a bite of it I couldn't open my mouth wide enough to take a bite and I started to cry because (he thought) I had lock jaw. He call the ship's doctor (Royce Pruet) and was told to give me a stick of gum which I chewed for about 30 minutes. After that I was able to eat but he would only give me a small bite or sometimes two small bites. It tasted like cake and ice cream to me when I was a child. When we got to where we could eat, they couldn't do enough. They kept asking questions if we would like some ice cream, some cake, or some sort of fruit, all the way to the Philippines.

We were taken good care of until we got to the hospital, so thanks to all the ship's crew. I never needed their help more and never appreciated it more than I did then and still do now. I didn't mean to write a book but thanks again for the way we were treated while aboard the USS Bassett.

/s/ Sherman C. Booth

Grover Carver   Spring 1998

Dear Peter:
It was with great interest I read your letter. You are correct in saying that too little is said of the Bassett and it is also true that the Bassett rescued the greatest number of survivors. I was one of the lucky ones as I was able to get aboard the boat that the four engine plane had dropped near us. There was a radio in the boat so we could communicate. We were informed that the nearest ship was 200 miles a way, so your ship must have "poured on the coal." I did not see your approach [probably sleeping]. Suddenly there was a search light illuminating our group and so very close. We saw the LCVP and the crew and they began to rescue us. We were transported to the Bassett and I climbed aboard. They asked me if I was okay to which I nodded, "Yes!" then I took

two steps and fell over the cargo wench. Two men grabbed me and put me on a stretcher. I was unable to talk but they read my lips and gave me a drink of water. I asked for more and after two large glasses my speech returned.

They put me in a bunk and asked if I was hungry. I responded, "Yes." They gave me an egg sandwich. I ate only about half as I was full, however I finished it later. In the morning I went to the mess hall for breakfast and I ate bread and butter with sugar on top. The doctor came to check me out and said that my food was a good choice. I was taken to the shower and two men helped me wash the bunker oil off. They gave me a pair of clean undershorts and a shirt. I do not believe your crew could have treated me and my fellow shipmates any better. Your crew was wonderful to us and extended their efforts to the fullest. I was still in shock and feared that a torpedo could hit the rescue vessel. I will never forget our rescue and I wish sometime to meet the sailors who took such good care of us. They are heroes to me.

/s/Grover Carver

Adolfo Celaya F-2/c Age 17 Survivor
Went aboard December 1944 direct from
San Diego Boot Camp

Telephone call from Celaya in the fall of 1997

Mr. Wren it is good to hear from you after all these years. Have often wondered why the USS Bassett never received the recognition that other ships in the rescue mission have. This is what I recall.

My friend Pena was a telephone talker on the bridge on the night of the sinking. When the watch changed he came down on the main deck to visit with me. When the torpedoes hit the ship it went down almost immediately. Together we jumped into the sea with only one life jacket between us. My friend Pena had the jacket and he shared it with me. We were able to get to an occupied raft and hung on to the outside ropes. Our arms were always extended upward and it became very tiresome but we hung on for the five days we were in the water. When the LCVP found us we were pulled aboard and then taken to the Bassett. The sea was very rough, the floor of the LCVP was very slippery, and I could not stand up so they brought me aboard in the wire basket.

When aboard the Bassett he remembers he received fresh water every time he asked for it but he cannot remember the orange slices or the lemonade. Celaya said he slept a lot. He was awakened in the shower with all his clothes cut off and someone cleaning him up. He received a pair of shorts and more drinking water. He continues to remember the rough sea, the wire basket and the canvas bunk where he didn't have to hang on.

Adolofo Celaya runs a heating and air conditioning business in San Diego, California and does speak before groups about his experience.

Chuck Gwinn, who first spotted the oil slick that led to the rescue was a neighbor and they have become great friends.

Loel Dean Cox   Fall 1998
USS Indianapolis Survivor

L.D.Cox sent me a tape from which I gleaned the following for your reading. Shipmate Cox was a telephone talker on the bridge on the night of the sinking. He was on the telephone circuit to the engine room.

When the first torpedo hit the ship, he was knocked off his feet and fell back on his stomach. Looking up he saw a

105

geyser of water higher than the deck he was standing on. A second explosion followed and he was thrown off his feet again and back on the deck. His telephone circuit was dead and he could not raise anyone on the line. The Captain who had taken his rest in the cabin near the navigation bridge came out and asked the Officer of the Deck what information he had. There was confusion on the lower decks as crewmen ran to their General Quarters stations. The Damage Control Officer reported to the Captain and said the situation was out of control and recommended that the Captain give the order to "Abandon Ship." The ship was taking a starboard list and Cox said he helped the Captain put on his life jacket. The life jackets were all brand new and had been put aboard before they left San Francisco. The list continued to grow to the starboard side and the word was passed to abandon ship. Cox said he left the ship from the port side and as usual he had his mouth open when he hit the water. He ended up with a big gulp of "bunker oil" and was wretching and throwing up for quite awhile. He swam about 75 yards from the ship and looked back to see the bow under water and the stern standing straight up with the propellers turning. Shipmates were jumping off the ship as best they could. Then all went dark; all this happened in about twelve minutes.

Cox had been on the ship since the fall season of 1944. He had participated in the Battle of Iwo Jima, the raid on Tokyo Bay and the Battle of Okinawa. The Indy was a great ship and now it was gone.

On the second day in the water he kicked his shoes off as they were weighing him down. An airplane flew over and they kicked, screamed and hollered, but it was of no avail as the airplane just continued on its way. Sharks circled below. They would pick off a mate and disappear in the waters below, never to reappear. Morale was very low and Cox said to himself, "If only two of us are picked up, I will be one of

106

them!" The sun, the sharks, and the lack of fresh water began to drive some of the shipmates out of their minds.

On the third day funny things began to happen. One of his shipmates asked everyone to be quiet. He said he was receiving a message on his radio from a submarine which was just below them. The submarine was going to surface and pick them up. Then he asked if anybody in the group wet the bed when he was younger. One man raised his hand and the mate told him he could not get aboard as the sub didn't allow that.

Another shipmate said the scuttlebutt (drinking fountain) was down on the second deck and he was going down to get a drink. He took off his life jacket and dove down. He never came back to the group.

After that Cox tied the knots on his life jacket very tight so that if he ever got to that state of mind he would not be able to get out of his jacket. They began to take the life jackets off the dead and give them to the men who had the belt type that you had to blow up. The belt type leaked air but they were too weak to blow up the belts.

Two officers in the group approached him saying, "There was a special island right over there and if Cox would guide them, they would talk to the island people to let him stay. It was an island for officers only." Cox said he took a few strokes from the group and advised the officers that he couldn't lead them and for them to come back to the group, but they swam away. He never saw them again.

He heard the PBY (a navy type float airplane) flying lower than the other airplanes that had flown by. They yelled and screamed and splashed the water, but it was of no avail. The PBY came back again and then circled lower for a third pass and they saw a man in the hatch door of the plane waving. Cox said, "My hair stood straight up!" The man threw a package and someone swam over to bring it back to the group. He thought it was fresh water but he doesn't remember if he received any.

On the fifth night (Friday morning) he woke up to have a bright light in his face and strong arms pulling him aboard a boat. He was taken to a ship and he was able to climb the rope ladder. He took three steps on the deck and fell flat on his face. They picked him up and put him in a bunk with a canvas bottom. He went sound asleep with his arms under his body. When he was awakened his arms were almost glued to the canvas. They had to pull his arms up from the canvas. [Note: Cox doesn't explain what caused this. Probably he had a severe burn on his stomach when he was blown off the deck by the first torpedo hit. He landed on his stomach.] He received tender loving care on the Bassett and was transferred Saturday morning to the Medical Facility on Samar. When in the medical facility on Samar, he said his stomach was wrapped in gauze and the nurses changed it frequently. He stayed there about two to three weeks. He learned from a nurse that the Indy had carried the atom bomb to Tinian and that it had been dropped on Hiroshima. He then realized what the secret cargo was that the Indy carried to Tinian. The nurse commented, "Maybe the war will end soon!" He was flown to a hospital in Guam and then to a Submarine Rest & Recreation area where he enjoyed lots of ice cream and where he played table tennis. Eventually he was transferred to the USS Hollandia and then returned to the states for discharge.

He was profusely thankful for his rescue by the Bassett and wants the crew and officers to know his feelings.

Tape from L.D. Cox

108

Harold W. Daniel CWO [retiree]   April 1998
Survivor

At the time of the rescue I was a Chief Boatswain Mate on the USS Indianapolis. The Chief Petty Officers on the Bassett were good sailors and they did everything that could have been done and more. Later I found out that fresh fruit was in short supply and the CPO mess readily gave its ration to the survivors. Further they assigned a mess cook to me. He had the tasks of getting me clean and getting plenty of liquids in me. He would bring me a glass of juice while I was in the shower. I would drink half of it and then fill it with the fresh water of the shower and gulp it down. He would then take my glass and go back for more juice. We were so dehydrated. I didn't get into a bunk until nearly 5:00 am. (All our boats were aboard by 5:16 am). What a sleep I had. I didn't awaken until we reached the Island of Samar in the Philippines. I was one of the more fortunate ones as I was ambulatory.

Harold W. Daniel wrote again 21 April 1998 with this to say.

As regards CBM Hines, I remember the incident quite well. He was on the port side of the main deck when I climbed aboard. Hines recognized me and turned to one of the seaman helping us and said, "Throw that one back!" And I said to him, "If he tries there will be three of us in the water, you, me and the seaman!" After that I was taken below to the CPO quarters. You know the rest of the story.

Sincerely
/s/ Harold W. Daniel

Joe E. J. Dronet's story
Survivor   Fall 1998

In Joe's correspondance with me he recites the
following: Joe was born 10 August 1927 in New Iberia, La.
and joined the US Navy on his 17th birthday. He spent three
month in San Diego Boot Camp and was assigned to the USS
Indianapolis December 1, 1944. He served in the Gunnery
Department aboard the ship participating in the air strikes on
Japan, the capture of Iwo Jima, and Okinawa where the Indy
was hit by a kamikaze suicide plane. On returning to the
Pacific after bringing the Atomic Bomb parts to Tinian and
while enroute to Leyte the Indy was sunk by a Japanese
submarine.

On that Sunday July 30 there appeared to be more
crewman desiring to go to church services than before. I
really don't know until today why. It seemed that something
was telling us to pray especially hard that day. The Catholics
were busy relieving the Protestants on watch so they could
attend their services and later the Protestants relieved the
Catholics so they could attend Mass. Joe was sleeping on the
forecastle that night near the 20 mm guns when an explosion
sent him about two feet into the air off the deck. He felt a
pain in his right foot, and when he touched it he felt blood.
He concluded it must have been shrapnel. The list to the
starboard side of the ship became very steep and he
eventually slid into the water when it was about ten feet from
him. He had put on his life jacket but admitted he wasn't
much of a swimmer and he knew he had to get away from the
ships drag as it was going down.

Dronet spotted a buddy from Oklahoma named
Cozell Smith, Jr. who, though he was short, he was a better
swimmer than Dronet. He hung on to Cozell and kicked hard
to get away from the ship's downward suction. Dronet said,
"We finally got away from the ship and when we looked back

110

all we could see was the aft part of the ship going down." They continued to swim and joined up with others. A life net had floated up and by count there were 124 men hanging on to it to stay afloat and be close together for there was safety in numbers. It wasn't until a Naval patrol airplane spotted an oil slick and came down close to sea level to inspect it that the men were discovered. On the fourth day afloat an aircraft dropped a life raft and other supplies near them.

Dronet continues, "But it wasn't until 3:00 am on the fifth day that we began to see search lights!" Dronet then fell asleep floating. When he awakened the searchlights came closer. [This could have been the battle lantern a crew member on the LCVP boat was holding on the survivors.] Dronet said he passed out as he was hauled on to a landing barge. Of the 124 men only 26 remained. Dronet was picked up by a rescue crew from the USS Bassett, which is the ship that went to the nearest Medical Facility at Samar Island, P.I. It was here that Joe celebrated his 18th birthday on August 10, 1945. After a convalesence in Guam he was granted a leave. Joe received the Purple Heart and has three stars on his Asiatic-Pacific ribbon. Dronet says, "I thank God for being one of the lucky survivors and for the miracle of our angel Chuck Gwinn for sighting us, also for Lt Adrian Marks and all the other rescue units. I often wonder what tale would have been told about the disappearance of the Indy had Chuck not spotted us."

/s/Joe Dronet

Dear Mr. Wren:

I, Harold Eck, served aboard the USS Indianapolis from December 1944 until the sinking on the night of 30 July 1945 just a few minutes after midnight.

I survived the most horrendous 108 hours in shark infested water. I watched in disbelief with shipmates badly burned, blinded, severely injured, covered with oil, moan in pain waiting for rescue.

I was rescued by the USS Bassett, the ship that picked up 152 dehydrated, delirious men covered with black oil and the ugliest ulcers ever known by man! When the small boat came near to pick me out of the water, I blacked out. I awakened briefly on board moaning in a wire basket, and passed out again until I awoke all cleaned, dry and safe, moaning for water. I was given an orange by a most kind sailor. The next time I regained consciousness I was in the hospital on the island of Samar.

I was told by a rescue officer that he had turned on a search light skyward. That light saved my life and helped me to muster up enough hope and courage to not give up.

I can't express the feelings I have for the USS Bassett and her great crew for our rescue and the splendid treatment. I would not have made it, as I was more dead than alive.

Very gratefully yours
/s/ Harold A Eck.

In his telephone call Buck recalls he was picked up by one of the LCVP's and thought it was a barge. As he lay in the bottom of the craft he remembers someone saying; "We will need a stretcher for this one!" He was hoisted up and placed on the fantail of the Bassett. Someone gave him a lit cigarette and he felt his lungs open. He was rolled on to a bunk and given a little water. He said he kept hiding the paper cup so he could get more water. He was treated with utmost kindness and remembers especially an African American was extraordinary helpful to him. Sometime later he was taken for a shower and remembers receiving more food and water. Once he was put into a bunk he knew he didn't have to hang on. Sleep was more important to him at this point as he had received food and water.

Any word he might utter would be inadequate to express his and other survivors' thanks. The Bassett crew were like "Angels of Mercy!"

Phone Call,

Buck Gibson

Thomas G. Goff
Survivor of USS Indianapolis   March 1999

Tom Goff ignored the fact that his occupation in an essential industry, and his age, would be enough to exempt him from military service. When he received his draft notice he didn't wait for the unusual "call-up" but enlisted in the US Navy to do his part.

Upon completion of his boot camp training he was assigned to the USS Indianapolis. After reporting aboard he found his sleeping quarters in the "A" [forward] section of the ship and two decks below the main deck. Sleeping down there was like being near the furnaces he worked near while making tires for Goodyear Tire Company. As a civilian he could cool off in the evenings in Ohio. Here in the tropics the sun baked the steel decks all day and then at night radiated that same heat down into the living compartments. The only cool place in the evening was out on the main deck of the Indy. The night before the sinking of the USS Indy he decided to sleep topside and enjoy the cool ocean breeze. It was a fortunate decision because at midnight the USS Indy was hit by two torpedoes and went down in 12 minutes. The first torpedo struck the area of Goff's bunk and the second hit midships. Those fortunate sailors who were able to scramble topside from their lower level quarters were wearing only their skivvys [t-shirt and shorts]. Those with presence of mind grabbed a life jacket, but with the starboard list so severe many just dove into the sea and swam away from the sinking ship.

Shipmates in the water gathered in large groups. Those without jackets or without the pneumatic belts were herded into the center of the groups and depended on those with floatation devices to support them until more jackets would float up from the sinking ship. The wounded and the badly burned were the first to succumb. Many didn't survive

114

the first night. The deceased sailors with pants and shirt were undressed and the clothes given to those in their skivvys. The deceased sailor would be pushed away from the group; the survivors had to watch the sharks attack the bodies. There was never any doubt of who would gain by one's death. Fear and panic raced through the group at every shark attack. The sun would burn them during the day and they would freeze at night.

The guy next to me thought the sea water was orange juice and drank hardily. It took only about three to four hours before he died. Of the group around me about 40 to 50 percent went crazy. One would look at another and think he was the enemy and start to fight. Most of the older men remained silent and tried to save their strength. Goff was rescued by the Bassett. Tom Goff says he takes only showers these days. He had all the time he will ever need soaking some fifty plus years ago!

/s/ Tom Goff

LCDR Lewis Haynes, MD
Survivor

This is the story that LCDR Lewis L. Haynes, Medical Corps, USN tells and this book would not be complete without it. My information comes from the TV-Discovery Channel aired in the fall of 1998. Doc Haynes is an Indy survivor.

Doc Haynes continued to practice good medicine while in the water with a group of survivors awaiting rescue. He talked to the men, trying to allay their anxieties, encouraging them to be brave and help each other. One of the most important disciplines everyone had to obey was to refrain from drinking the salt water, because it just increased their thirst. Secondly, they were to check on each other through the night and to answer roll call in the morning. If a shipmate didn't respond in the morning, the nearest man to him was to call out to the doctor so he could check on the sailor failing to report.

The doctor would try to awaken the silent one and if he proved to have died during the night, the Doc would unhook his life jacket and let him slowly drift away and sink. The Doc would then call on everyone to recite with him the "Lords Prayer." This prayer may have been the ingredient necessary for their survival. Had they not survived and had the doctor not lived to tell us about this we would never have been able to record it in this book. During WWII there was a saying "There are no atheists in the fox holes!" and the same truth can be applied in the open sea. Doc Haynes says to this day he cannot recite the "Lord's Prayer" without tears.

Ltr from Clarence L. Hershberger
Survivor of the USS Indianapolis

6 March 1998

Dear Mr Wren:

Enclosed is the 27 page booklet of my memories of that night in August 1945. 1 hope in some small way this maybe of help in your development of your book on the USS Bassett. Use it wisely and in good faith.

Sincerely,

/s/ClarenceL. Hershberger.

Clarence's book recounts his experience after five days in the Philippine Sea. From his writings I have taken some of the more poignant parts which readily reflect the character and strength of this sailor who had served 14 months on the Indy and who did his part to help win the ten campaign medals Indy earned. Clarence wrote that on three different occasions he felt the presence of the Lord and he shares them with us.

THE FIRST. Clarence had gone topside on the Indy to sleep on the night of 29 July 1945 because it was so stifling hot below deck in the berthing area. He had his blanket and was walking around on the darkened ship, but he had trouble finding a place to sack out. A good number of the crew had the same idea and just walking about the deck was difficult because he didn't want to step on someone asleep. The fantail had too much vibration from the turning propeller blades of the ship so he went forward and found a spot under the number one gun on the foc'sle. He bunked down next to the hatch that led to the ammunition magazine below. The first torpedo hit the bow at about midnight and the explosion threw him about three feet off the deck. The second torpedo hit about midships and was followed by an explosion in the forward magazine. When he returned to the deck from his imprompt flight he had a sheet of fire all around him and a large red glow from the hatch he had just bunked near.

Though in mortal danger with fire all around him, he was soaking wet as though a wave had washed over him, but he cannot recall any such wave. He felt the presence of the Lord and walked toward the rear of the ship unscathed.

THE SECOND. The second presence of the Lord was felt when he and his ship mate Cleatus LeBow looked down into the clear blue water at a large shark just below their legs. While others screamed "SHARK" and beat on the water he felt the "calmness" of the Lord's presence and the shark disappeared as quickly as he had appeared.

THE THIRD. He felt the presence of the Lord when Chuck Gwinn's plane flew over them even though the survivors were scattered over several miles of the Philippine Sea. Again a calmness came over him and he knew rescuers were coming.

In his writings, Clarence invites all who may have lost a loved one in this war, or any war, to stop by the wonderful Memorial in Indianapolis and find closure for your loved ones. Be they lost at sea, buried in a foreign land, or in an unknown grave or simply still missing, use the Memorial for a final "Good Bye" if you wish, and use it lovingly. Further he asks that all the children and grandchildren of the survivors of the USS Indianapolis understand the bonding of the crew and that they, the children, become the "Second Watch." The "Second Watch" would be an organization of second and third generation persons of the original survivors. He requests that they take over when the survivors can no longer continue the prayers for those lost at sea and for peace.

Further, on the night of his rescue he recites the following. "Suddenly there were electric lanterns shining in our faces causing us to open our eyes. We saw a landing craft looming beside us. The fellows in the landing craft were leaning over the side and reaching out to us. We could hardly believe it, we were finally being rescued.

"Now I'm not certain of the exact time that I was helped from the water into the landing craft, but I am certain that it was early morning because it was still dark. After arriving aboard the USS Bassett, help and care were given with great generosity. Rank on the Bassett must have been set aside, to a large degree, from the moment the first survivors were brought aboard. It wasn't unusual to see a first class gently sponging the oil off a survivor's body and hair, while a seaman held a glass of juice for the survivor. Others were disposing of our oil soaked clothes. Another Bassett crew member was assisting the doctor, while another was scrounging up clean clothes for us to wear. It was "Amazing Grace" for sure.

"While we were being cleaned up and checked out by the doctor, we were asked what we would like to eat. Now, while I'm sure there were comedians in our group of survivors, I was surprised to hear one of my shipmates ask for steak and a baked potato. I don't think that's what he got but he did ask for it. Some of my shipmates asked for and received soup, but the biggest request was for ice cream. For the most part we were allowed to sleep and when we did wake up by chance, a crew member was right at our elbow asking what would we like or what he could do for us. It was like being a King for the Day on that day.

"After spending about a week in the base hospital on Samar, we were mustered together one morning and taken to a nearby airfield. We were placed aboard a C-47 cargo plane which flew us to Guam. Here we joined the rest of the survivor group and learned only 317 of the estimated 880 who abandoned ship had come out of it alive.

"It would be around 1990 that the Navy Department released the information on the tragedy and the events that followed. There will probably always be some unanswered questions. Even the blemish on our skipper's service record remains. He was made the scapegoat for the many mistakes that were made in the Navy's chain of command which only add to the coverup that took place. At our fifty year anniversary reunion in 1995 and Memorial dedication, the two Navy representatives admitted, in private, that our Captain's court martial should never have happened. Good! Then why not admit it publicly and put the whole matter to rest."

Clarence Hershberger - booklet

George Horvath   Spring 1998
Indy Survivor

George writes as follows:

I was in a whaleboat [which was] dropped by a B-17. When one of your LCVP's picked me and others up, we were transported to the Bassett. Along side the Bassett I was helped up a rope ladder and able to stand on the fantail of the Bassett. I was led to the shower and with the aid of some kind of oil and soap I was cleansed.

Someone from the Bassett helped me shampoo my head with more of the same oil and soap. After the shower I was given lots of orange juice and put in a bunk were I crapped out. I believe I slept all the way to Samar with time out to eat. "J.C." Phillips of the Bassett crew outfitted me with clothes, and to this day I still have his white hat!

/s/George Horvath

Ltr from James K. Jarvis   February 20, 1999
Indy survivor

Dear Mr Wren:

I was inducted into the US Navy in January 1944.
After boot camp in Sampson, NY, Aviation Sheet Metal
School in Norman, Oklahoma, and Advanced Base Training
at Providence, RI, I was sent to CAS V6 at the Alameda Air
Station in Alameda, California. I was then transferred to the
SOS V3 at the same base. From there I was sent to Memphis,
Tenn. for specialized training on the SC-1 planes which were
being deployed on the USS Indianapolis. In April 1945 1 was
assigned to the Indianapolis which was being repaired at
Mare Island after being hit by a Kamikaze off Okinawa. In
July we took a short shake down cruise and then picked up a
box marked "Radio Gear" at Hunters Point, San Francisco,
Calif.

We then went to Pearl Harbor and from there to
Tinian where we dropped off the "Radio Gear" box. We did
wonder about the "Box" since there was a Marine guard on it
24 hours a day. Also, I heard the Boatswain Mate say, if it
had weighed another 100 lbs more it would have been beyond
the capacity of our crane. We thought that was awfully heavy
for radio gear, but we had no idea what it was. The box was
in the port hangar where I bunked and we would walk on it
to service the plane in the hangar. We finally found out what
it was when coming back from Peleliu to Guam on the USS
Tranquility when it was announced that an Atomic Bomb was
dropped on Hiroshima.

After dropping off the "Box" at Tinian we went to
Guam and picked up supplies and ammunition. We left for the
Philippines and were about half way there when we were
sunk. I was asleep on the mezzanine of the port hangar when
the torpedoes hit. I don't know if the jar from the explosion

121

woke me up or that it was so quiet when the air intake fans for the ship's ventilation fans quit. These fans were so noisy you could barely talk to anyone in the hangar. When I woke up I could see sparks coming down on the welldeck and into the hangar. This was the only fire I saw. I tried to find my inflatable life jacket belt which I kept by my bunk with a sheath knife on it, but the jar from the explosion must have moved it. I then grabbed a kapok life jacket, helmet and gas mask and went down into the well deck. The ship was listing to starboard. The water was about half way across the well deck. Since it was so hard to stand on the deck we decided to get off. I took off my helmet, climbed over the port rail, scooted down into the water and started swimming to get away from the suction caused by the sinking ship. Most of the "V" division, which took care of the planes, got off about the same time so we were in the same group in the water. We were not too concerned because we thought a big ship like that would surely be missed. We were lucky to be in warm water. In the North Atlantic you survived only for a few minutes.

The next day wasn't so bad except for the sun beating down on our heads. I used my pocket knife to cut off one pant leg to pull over my head. Our faces were protected somewhat by the thick coating of bunker oil. I didn't see any shark attacks. Only saw one big fish which could have been a shark. By Tuesday we were getting more concerned about our situation and by Wednesday some of the men were hallucinating about the ship being just a few feet under the water and would try to dive down to it. I moved away from the group with H.L. Hopper. He came from Muncie, Indiana and was a good friend. We were both in the Aviation Sheet Metal rates. Sometime on Wednesday Hopper decided we should both try to swim to Leyte. Anyone in their right mind would know how impossible it would be to swim 300 miles. He almost had me convinced but I finally decided not to go.

The last I saw of him was his head above a wave a few hundred feet away.

I stayed away from the group until Thursday when we were spotted by Wilbur Gwinn. By this time we were really thirsty. At first you get hungry; but when you get thirsty you forget about being hungry. We all called Wilbur Gwinn "Our Angel." If he had not spotted us while on a routine patrol, probably none of us would have survived. His crew dropped all their survival equipment to us. He then circled over us until Adrian Marks' PBY arrived. Gwinn had only enough fuel left to return to his base. One of the five man inflatable rafts was dropped close to our group. Dr. Haynes got on the raft and took as many of the ones in the worst shape that he could get onto it. There was some water and medical supplies on the raft that Dr. Haynes used for the ones in the worst shape. I didn't get any of the water and I didn't need any of the medical supplies.

Wilbur Gwinn reported our position and in a short time the PBY piloted by Adrian Marks arrived. After seeing the condition we were in he decided to land on the sea and pick up as many as he could. The plane was several hundred yards from me so I decided not to try to swim to it. I did think how great it would be to get my feet on something sound. It is very uncomfortable to have your feet and legs dangling for that length of time. Some of the ones on the raft died which made room for some of us in the water. I got on the raft after dark on Thursday evening. There were nine of us on a five-man raft including Dr. Haynes. We could see the search lights from the USS Doyle so we knew help was on the way.

I had been on the raft for a while when I heard someone in the water call, "Hey Jarvis!" One of the men on the raft said, "that's a Destroyer." I said, "No, that's Ashford." I called to him so he could tell where we were, and he came paddling up with his arms over his life belt. All of the cement on his straps had come off and all that was left was a long cylinder which he was hanging on. He was John T Ashford from Lubbock, Texas and was our Radio Technician for the aircraft. Later that night the USS Doyle picked us up. We were covered with oil but they put us in their bunks and took us to Peleliu.

From there we went to Guam on the USS Tranquility, [hospital ship]. After a few weeks in the hospital and a Submarine Rest Base we returned to San Diego, California on the USS Hollandia [small carrier]. From there we received a 30 day survivors leave. I returned to Alameda Air Station and then transferred to the Fifth Naval District in Norfolk, Va. with a short stay in Elizabeth City, NC. I was discharged in May 1946.

My family and I hope to attend the Reunion this summer. We will try to see you then.

/s/ Jim Jarvis

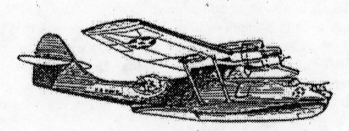

Consolidated PBY "Catalina"

{Note: Joe Kiselica sent me a 27 page write up he produced and gave me permission to used as much as I needed to tell the story.}

Joe was on the hangar deck where the two scout planes are housed and was finishing up working on one of the planes. He thought he would go below for the sandwiches available for the ongoing watch. But because it was so hot below he changed his mind and pulled down the foldup wall cot and quickly dozed off. The first torpedo hit forward and was followed quickly by the second which struck about midships. Kiselica was literally blown out of his cot and saw men running to their battle stations. Fire from below with muffled explosions was followed by more fire and explosions. Flames were coming from every opened hatchway. In an effort to slow down the list now developing, hatches were closed, trapping the men below to an ignited hell. All communication systems were out of order and the list increased as the ship plunged downward. Later Kiselica learned that Captain McVay had asked the bugler to blow "Abandon Ship" but the bugler misunderstood the order, dropped his bugle and jumped over the side.

Men with life jackets tried to loosen the life rafts from their moorings but the list of the ship wedged the rafts tight. The propellers continued to turn, driving the ship into a dive. Those who had escaped the fire breathing hatches and those who were injured by the explosive blasts were jammed into life jackets and pushed over the sides. Some of the badly burned screamed not to be touched. Melting skin hung in pouches from bodies. The stench of burning flesh was unbearable. Kiselica tied life jackets on any part of the body of a wounded mate and helped him get over the side. The

125

ship lurched 90 degrees to the starboard making all decks vertical to the water. Kiselica grabbed a life jacket and ran barefooted over the now exposed port side and right into the water.

Now being water borne he looked up to see the ship's two propellers still turning with the stern elevated and plunging into the sea. The men on the fantail leaped to avoid the propellers. All went dark and he swam away. At twelve minutes after midnight the Indy was gone.

At dawn on the 30th of July 1945, Kiselica counted about 150 shipmates and he estimated about 100 more that were wounded and injured without life jackets had slipped between the waves during the night hours. By morning Kiselica said he was rising and falling between eight to ten foot waves. His eyes stung from the salt water spray and the bunker fuel oil. He made himself vomit up the oil scum and sea water he had swallowed. Everyone near him was puking. Then he began to see and hear what he never wants to see and hear again.

A figure floated toward him. It was a body with its face blown off and only a tongue hanging out of where the throat should be. Somehow the guy was still alive. There was nothing he could do to help him. Suddenly the figure slumped forward and was dead. He said a prayer from him, "May God rest his soul!" There were parts of human bodies all around me and they began to attract sharks. All through that morning's darkness I heard terrible screams as sharks attacked. I can still hear those screams.

In the process of sinking the propellers continued to turn and groups of survivors were scattered. But we knew if we stayed in a large group we would be easier to find. We formed a circle and kept the wounded and the badly burned and those without life jackets in the center. They were going crazy with pain but here was nothing we could do about it.

The first act of survival was to remove our water logged shoes as they weighed us down. Another mate's arm was hanging by a piece of muscle. He was screaming in agony. A bunch of us held him while another mate with a pen knife cut his arm off He died that night. We all felt that when the ship failed to report Tuesday at 11:30 am at Leyte they would send rescue ships and planes to find us. We just had to hang on for a few more hours.

Taking a look around on the third morning after the sinking we could see about half of the 150 men were still there. First we cursed the Japs and then the Navy for not coming. After a while the Japs were not the enemy. It was the tropical sun and the sea. A blazing tropical sun caused a glare on the sea, which I learned later is called "photophobia." The glare burns the eyes whether closed or not making the eyes feel as though they had hot pokers in them. To defend from the hot glaring sun the sailors tore off their shirt tails and blindfolded themselves, others made improvised hats to shield their eyes. Others just smeared the bunker oil all over their faces and heads. One sailor had a rosary and lead us in prayers, bead by bead, over and over again. Members of every faith joined in. If you had never prayed before you learned then. Many prayed to die. It was easier than to try to stay alive,

With life jackets holding you only at chin level, the cool water became very tempting to drink and some convinced themselves a little sip wouldn't hurt. "You bastards," I yelled at them, "you're gonna die if you drink that water!" I was tempted to take a sip just like everyone else. Some men you could control. Some you couldn't and their liquid refreshment lasted only a short while. The first thing you noticed after an hour or so was that they would start mumbling. Later they would start thrashing around like crazy. You couldn't hold them. Then they would have to keep drinking more and more to stop the fires in their bellies. Their tongues would begin to swell until they could hardly breathe. Then they would begin choking to death. It would take them three to four hours to die.

Another problem was the life jackets which because of their canvas construction, became a source of chafing under the arms and around the neck. Bunker oil would help but it also burned the open salt water sores. The jackets were made for about 72 hours of bouyancy. The jackets were now sinking lower and lower into the sea and fights would break out over jackets. Kiselica said, "I recall holding one guy for hours not knowing he was dead. When I turned him I saw he had only half a body. The lower half had been eaten by the sharks. With help from others we slipped the life jacket off and gave it to a mate whose jacket needed to be replaced.

Sharks circled us day and night and I will never forget the sight of their wide rolling eyes. They attacked the bleeding and the wounded and always preferred the lone targets. Yelling and shouting didn't seem to bother them; they just got bolder and bolder. We were nothing but bait to them. You never knew when it would be your turn. It was a horrible way to die. Small sharks liked to take nibbles and nips out of you, then the large sharks would come up and rip the body apart. There were screams and more screams. As long as the fin was visible you didn't have to worry. When the fin coming at you disappeared below the surface then you would tense up and wait for the hit. Joe said all the time he was in the water all the sharks did was to bump him and scrape his legs and feet. There were other fish to fear such as the barracuda and the jelly fish who would nip or sting you.

Kiselica continues his story. A lot of these sailors in the water were age 18 and under. We always called them cookie sailors because we knew their mothers or girl friends would be sending them cookies and they would share with us.

Some men began hallucinating. Fights broke out with the stronger men challenging the weaker ones. Some thought the Japanese frog men were coming to kill them and began to attack one another. Some swam off for a beautiful tropical island with a "posh" hotel they visioned. Some believed the USS Indy was floating just down below with casks of fresh water. They would pull off their life jackets, dive down for a drink and never return. I was tempted to swim off to one of those island places. The guy next to me belted me across the chops. I asked him why he did that and he said that, I had swiped his car keys. Later that day Orsburn punched me in my face yelling, "You bastard, you cut off my long distance call to my mom in Arkansas!" It was my turn to calm him down. We were all going nuts.

On Wednesday, August 1, there were only 75 of the 150 left on the net. On Thursday morning Joe said he could count only 30 men left hanging on. Another day he thought would end it all. Sharks continue to attack. Water logged life jackets began to drown the men who couldn't get out of them. It was on this day that Wilbur Guinn saw the ribbon of oil on the sea and came lower to investigate the oil slick and saw black figures waving at him. He then radioed his base on Palau Island of his observations and his position. Guinn circled around the black figures in the water and dropped his life raft containing emergency rations and his life jackets. Meanwhile Lt Marks loaded his PBY Catalina with survival gear and took off from Palau Island. Enroute to the location Lt. Marks flew over the USS Doyle and advised the skipper LCDR W. Graham Clayton, Jr., that there were men in the water 200 miles ahead of him. Kiselica remembers the plane [Guinn's] circled him again and again. Joe goes on to say, " If Guinn hadn't seen that oil slick none of us would have survived. It was a miracle when I first saw that airplane. I thought I was dreaming. Some of us didn't seem to care; we were too far gone. We were too weak to go after the supplies that were dropped. We just had to hang on a little longer."

Kiselica continues, "When I first saw those beams of light low and far on the horizon, I thought I had died and was going to go to heaven on one of those beams. Then I realized it must be a ship. If we could just hang on for another night, we might make it. We must not sleep. We must keep our faces out of the water for one more night. We kept pulling each other's hair, and punching each other to stay awake. More ships arrived and soon the place was lit up like a circus. We could hear the bull horns from the launches calling to us. We were too far gone to call back." Kiselica and Orsburn were part of the group of 11 that were picked up by the USS Talbot on Friday at about 7:30 AM. [Note: The USS Bassett had already left at 6:00 am for the Med-Center on Samar Island with 152 survivors] The rescuers had a difficult time handling the survivors as seared flesh pulled away from their arms as they tried to recover them. Kiselica and his mates were carried up the rope ladder to the deck of the Talbot. Their skin was so soft that the bones poked through their feet. They suffered from sunburn, salt water ulcers, inflamation of the nose and throat, dehydration and pneumonia. Chunks of flesh were missing from parts of their bodies from the fish bites. Some of the men from the Talbot were crying when they saw us. Every opening in your body was infected one way or another including your genitals, your eyes, your ears, and your rectum.

When they announced that the first Atomic Bomb was dropped on Hiroshima on August 6th, and that the bomb was flown over Japan from Tinian by the B-29 known as the Enola Gay, a loud cheer went up in the Hospital Ward. Finally we knew what our secret cargo was. It was our ship that was chosen for the mission that would shorten the war. It was a good feeling after all that had happened.

Dear Peter:

On the night of the sinking I felt as though I had a high fever so I crawled up on the fantail to sleep. I thought I was going to die if I stayed in my bunk. My buddy McKlin joined me on the fantail and we bedded down for the night. Your ship saved me and my shipmate, Santos Pena, an Arizona boy who is still living.

We were on a floater net for five whole days in the water. We had five nets tied together. We counted one by one and I remember we had 187 men hanging on to those nets. Only 16 survived that ordeal. When we were rescued by the Bassett, Edward Kizer of Cobbs Creek, Va. helped me by cutting off my oil soaked clothing and took my identification metal tags for safe keeping. I have no recollection that he had saved them. We called them "dog tags." Kiser planned to return them before Lopez got off the Bassett, but when the ship arrived at the Samar Medical Facility, Kizer must have been on watch and Lopez knew nothing about the safe keeping of his "dog tags."

All these years Kiser has had Lopez's "dog tags' with the intention of returning them some day. All these years Lopez felt the tags were at the bottom of the Philippine Sea. In July of 1995 the USS Indianapolis Memorial was dedicated in Indianapolis, Indiana. Ed Kiser learned a neighbor was at the dedication. Kiser called him and spoke of Lopez's "dog tags" which he had saved waiting to return them someday. His neighbor had a listing of the survivors who had attended and Lopez's name and address were listed in the program. Kiser phoned Sam Lopez saying, "He had some personal belongings of a Sam Lopez who was a survivor of the USS Indianapolis. Was this the Sam Lopez?" Of course, the answer was "Yes!" What a surprise and what a great guy to follow up on his small matter after all these years.

/s/ Sam Lopez

Ltr from Robert A. Lucas   Summer 1998
Rescued by the Bassett

On July 30, 1945, 1 was standing gunwatch below the bridge. When the first blast came I was knocked down on the deck. I got up to see what had happened and walked toward the front of the ship. I saw the bow blown off and went to get life jackets to put on the wounded.

The ship started to sink. All the wounded slipped down and forward. Somebody said, "Abandon Ship!" I made it down to the deck and jumped into the water and started to swim away from the ship. Someone said, "There she goes," and we all stopped and watched her go down.

The rest of the night and morning we looked for men from our division. There were men all over. The men that were in good shape looked after the men who drank the salt water and were sick, and also helped the men who were hurt on the ship before it went down. Every day there were more empty jackets floating around. After the second day we started to change life jackets. If a jacket was high in the water it was empty.

I don't know if it was the third or fourth day when we were spotted and the planes started to come. A PBY landed on the water and picked up men. A plane dropped a life jacket with clean drinking water in it. I went to get it. Going was easy. Coming back I was going against the current. I couldn't make it back. I had to let the water go. I was tired and I didn't think could get back. Then I heard a loud noise and looked up. There was a B-17 coming right at me. He

132

dropped a life raft right close to me. I was able to get it and climb in. A little later 6 or 7 men came to the raft. It was now dark and we worried that nobody would find us. All at once lights were coming our way. A boat came and took us off the raft. When we got to the ship and got aboard a man took our names. They gave us water and a bath and put us in bunks. The men on the ship took real good care of us.

/s/Robert Lucas

Ltr from H. Jay Miner II
Indy Survivor   23 February 1998

Dear Peter:

If you would like an on the spot report of how we felt about you guys, the following is a direct quotation from a letter I wrote my parents from the hospital in Samar, dated August 30, 1945.

Dear Mom and Dad:

Paragraph #3---We were spotted that morning and the planes were really buzzing around by mid-afternoon. For some reason that did not impress me much. I would have been hurt if they hadn't. I just floated there like a jelly-fish watching the boats and supplies being dropped to us. I was too tired to move, but not to notice the way things were being bungled. The guys in the boats wouldn't help those in the water or pass out drinking water, etc.

Evening came and we were still there. The one remaining Radio Technician and myself were telling each other that our troubles were over. Only hang on for a few more hours and we'd be picked up. Finally he cracked. He came up behind and me and threw his arms around my neck and would not let go. He said they had taken his life jacket and were trying to kill him. I got my life jacket around him

133

and then the nightmare started. [I dreamed] we were picked up and I buried my face in the sparkling scuttlebutt, [drinking fountain] and the clear bubbling water turned out to be salt. I woke up again and Ray was beside me and crying and again without a jacket. I shoved another one into his arms and cursed him wildly. He unsettled me completely. Whether dream or reality I don't know, but this was the worst of all. He was unconscious and I was trying to hold his head out of the water but he kept slipping down, down, down. I yelled at everyone near me to help for a moment, but no one looked up. He finally slipped loose and I could feel him bump my feet on the way down.

We were picked up about four [from what I read now it was probably earlier than four o'clock] the next morning. The few hours between when I lost Ray and when the APD found us were a mixture of dreams and truth. Each fantasy was worse than the preceding one. The second I felt that deck under me I just gave up all efforts. They poured a thin stream of cold water on my face and nothing has ever felt so good. The crew treated us magnificently. The crew gave up sleep for a couple of nights and devoted all their time to us. They all had huge beards. It must have looked mighty strange to see great bearded guys gently squeezing an orange into my mouth or holding my head up for a glass of water. They gave me two pints of plasma, but some of the guys were able to walk and eat.

At Samar they greeted me with an IV. In a couple more days I stood up a while and soon was able to eat and talk. I was one big mess of pimples, boils, ulcers, sunburn and oil. Anyhow, I'm okay now and I'll relate the rest of the story in my next letter. Hope this will go on two stamps.

All my love /Jack
{end of letter}

134

Miner continues:

Further to the above, I still have a fairly clear recollection of the few hours before you actually pulled us out of the water. Four or five us had, somehow, commandeered a life raft and were in it. When we saw your searchlight [from the LCVP, I guess], we decided you must be Japs, coming to machine gun us in the water. We mustered the last drops of energy in our bodies to get out of the life raft, hang on to the rear, and kick with all our strength to get away from the light. Fortunately, we probably didn't have the strength among us to move the raft faster than a few feet per hour. You caught us quickly. I remember being dragged into the LCVP, and taken aboard the ship. I'll never forget the tender, loving care with which you got me cleaned up in the shower, using diesel oil to dissolve the old oil in which I was encrusted. My stay aboard the USS Bassett was better than any 5-star hotel I've visited since.

In another letter Jay Miner writes: I started my naval career on my 18th birthday, March 7, 1944, and after completing one semester at Yale University, I was sent through boot camp and then to the Radio Technician School. I finished in the spring of 1945 as a Radio Technician 2/c. On or about July 1, 1945 I was assigned to the USS Indianapolis, then in dry-dock at Mare Island, California, where the ship was being repaired after having received kamikazi damage at Okinawa. We went to sea on July 16, were torpedoed on July 30 and rescued in the early morning of August 4. So my sea duty of WWII amounted to about 17 days, of which 13 days were aboard ship and the balance up to my chin in the ocean. Our rescue ship was the USS Bassett which took us to the medical facility on Samar Island of the Philippine Islands. After a few days I was flown to Guam, first, to testify before CINCPAC [Commander in Chief, Pacific], a board consisting of Commanders, Captains and Admirals--all very intimidating

135

to a second class petty officer--and second, to recuperate at a rest camp for the Submarine Forces with unlimited sleep and ice cream. Then home for a survivor's leave, a trip to Washington DC to testify at the Pentagon, and then back out to the Pacific for radio duty on Carlson's Island, a suburb of the Island of Kwajalein. The war ended and I was returned to civilian life in June of 1946 having completed a little better than two years of naval service.

THE MESSAGE

Herbert J. Miner, Indianapolis survivor
writes his recollections as follows: February 1998

     While we were in the water, I went through the same
fear, thirst, and general misery and dementia as the rest of our
bunch, perhaps 200 men the first night and 100 men the last
night. There was one unique part played by me during this
drama that made me slightly different from the rest, namely a
"certainty" that we would be picked up. Right after the
torpedoes hit we radio technicians assembled in Radio 2,
where all the radio transmitters were located. Radio 1 is the
main radio shack, where all messages were normally sent and
received. There were 7 or 8 of us and we had no idea what
had happened or what to do next. It was a little after
midnight, and most of us had been asleep. Within a short time
we were joined by Mr. Wood, our boss, and a Warrant
Officer. He was burned and covered with soot, but
thoroughly in command of the situation. He had been sleeping
in the forward part of the ship, near where the first torpedo
had hit. He knew that the cables connecting Radio I with
Radio 2 had been severed, so no messages could be sent from
Radio 1.

     He told me to warm up a certain transmitter and then
he told all of us to inflate our life belts and to put them on. He
then began to send an SOS message by using an emergency
key attached to the transmitter. I know the message went out
because I stood right beside him and watched the needle jump
in the power meter of the antenna circuit. I cannot remember
how long he keyed--maybe 15 seconds or maybe two
minutes--I don't know. When he had finished, the ship had
rolled at least 20 degrees to starboard, the direction we were
facing and it was almost impossible to stand. He gave the
"abandon ship" order. By the time I turned around the radio

shack was empty. As rapidly as I could, I left the shack and crawled down a ladder [stairs] to the main deck and abandoned ship. Then the four days of horror began, but I knew that a distress message had been sent and that we would be found. I believed that my certainty of rescue gave me the little edge that assured my survival. I passed the word to all the men around me, making a major effort to keep up morale. Of course, no one ever received the radio message, or if they did, it was never admitted. I am the only survivor of Radio 2, leaving no one to corroborate my story.

To what do I attribute my survival? The above mentioned radio message, of course, but the three chief reasons were luck, luck and luck. For example, my bunk was located about three levels below the main deck. If I had been in it, I would still be there. A few days before the sinking, my mattress had been stolen. Rather than sleep on the bare springs, I was able to set up a cot in Battle 2, a command post to be used in the event that Battle I [on the bridge] became unusable. Battle 2 was located just forward of Radio 2. The two rooms formed a "doughnut" around the after stack above the main deck. When the torpedoes hit I was two steps from Radio 2. Another example: when I reached the main deck while abandoning ship I was on the "wrong" side. The ship was rolling to the starboard side and I could be trapped under the hull as it rolled over. In trying to get to the port [high] side I grabbed the leg of a shipmate who had already begun to cross over to the port side, and I tried to pull myself up to get a new hand hold. Well, this shipmate would have none of it. With a curse, he kicked me loose, and I slid down the deck and directly into the water without much of a splash. The timing was such that the low [starboard] side was awash just as I reached it. I swam away as fast as I could. When I stopped for a breath, I turned to watch the silhouette of the ship, which had turned turtle silently slip out of sight, bow first. Additional factors were: I was barely 19 years old, and thanks special war time training at my high school and college, I was in top notch physical condition; I was a good swimmer and had no fear of water. Life had treated me well up until then, probably much better than I deserved, and I strongly wanted to continue living.

What did I think about when I was in the water? Foremost were thoughts related to basic survival. These included keeping my socks on so sharks wouldn't bite, keeping a piece of shirt around my head for protection from the sun, keeping my good eye [the other was clogged with fuel oil] out of the water, resting on the life net when squares became available, avoiding men who had gone beserk sooner than I, and wondering why the many planes that flew overhead did not appear to see us. I did try to help shipmates who weakened sooner than I. I fantasized about meeting my parents at a dim roadside bar in the north woods of Wisconsin to share the story over a few very cold beers. I bargained with God. As the days dragged on I thought less and less while I dreamed more and more during moments of fitful sleeping.

In all the intervening years, I've had only the nightmare once of that dying friend slipping out of my grasp and slowly sinking through the crystal clear water until he faded from sight. One dream like that is enough.

/s/ Herbert J. Miner

Ltr from Paul J. Murphy

USS INDIANAPOLIS CA 35
Survivors Organization
1205 West Avenue
Broomfield, CO 80020
February 7, 1997

L. Peter Wren
USS Indianapolis Rescue Crew Member

Dear Peter:

Thank you for your copy of the letter you sent to Jimmy O'Donnell. Isn't he a wonderful man! He has done so much for our organization and he is very special to all of us.

I would like to spend some time with you and talk about the rescue you accomplished. You saved my life.

All I can remember after the pickup was that I could not climb the ladder and your crew put me in a wire basket and hauled me aboard the USS Bassett. Another thing I remember is your white interior of the ship soon turned black and the oranges. WOW, did they ever taste good.

Yes your reunion is scheduled the same time as ours. Hope to see you in July. Please look me up.

Our committee will be meeting in March to finalize the reunion. Your name has been added to the list of "Rescue crew members" and is also on our mailing list. Jack Paul and Earle Houghtaling are the coordinators for your group and I have highlighted their addresses on the list enclosed.

See you in July. God bless you.

Smooth sailing
/s/ Paul J. Murphy

Dear L. Peter:

Don' t know if anyone has told you about the bucket of diesel oil that was used in the shower room to get the thick bunker oil out of the hair of the survivors. One of the survivors who insisted on helping himself was kneeling down on the shower deck with his head in the bucket of diesel oil. He lost his balance, and he was thrashing his head around in the bucket as he could not get his balance on the oil and water soaked deck. In view of all the misery the other survivors were enduring in the shower room as ship's crew tried to clean their bodies from the bunker oil, the sight of a shipmate wrestling around on the floor with a bucket on his head brought on a hilarious moment. It was quite funny, and I remembered I was laughing before we finally pulled his head out of the bucket.

I also remember when one of the your LCVP's came up. I thought it was the Japs arriving so I was walking and splashing around on the raft trying to fight your rescue efforts. When suddenly it dawned on me that you were pulling away with my shipmates and leaving me. So I called out to you to "Wait for me! " They took me aboard the LCVP and when we got up to the Bassett they asked me if I could climb the rope network. I said I didn't think so. They loaded me into a basket and hauled me aboard. What a wonderful feeling to have a deck under my feet!

/s/ Eugene S. Morgan

James O'Donnell, Indy survivor   Fall 1997
Source: oral history and a News article from the
Harrison Post 27 July 1997entitled
"Never Give Up" by Chris Calkins.

        At the 1997 reunion of the Indianapolis crew, the
USS Bassett crew was able coordinate their reunion at the
same time. In talking with Jim O'Donnell, I told him as rescue
officer in one of the LCVPs on that night I hadn't seen any
sharks and I was curious about the shark attacks. Our
conversation went like this, "Jim," I asked, "how did you
know there were sharks in the area around you? Were they
breaking the surface, and pulling men down? Just how did
you know?" His answer was that he was stepping on their
backs. He couldn't pull his legs up because the life jacket
restricted his leg movement. His legs could come up only so
far. It was a hell of a feeling wanting to get your feet and legs
out of the way and you couldn't. He said, "like the others
there in the water, we were frightened beyond all belief. And
still they came and still we could feel them under our feet. We
would kick our legs, thrash the water with our arms and yell
with all our might--SHARKS-SHARKS. Everyone would go
crazy trying to scare them away. I can't recall how many
times it occurred but it drove us into panic!"
        Sharks are attracted to body fluids blood and
excrement. The injured survivors were trailing blood and if
they have been gulping salt water they could be producing
body fluid through their diarrhea. Sharks are also attracted by
abnormal underwater sounds such as a sinking ship. Jim
O'Donnell's rescue experience is as follows:
        "I had about four hours to sleep before I went on
watch. I was sleeping on the top deck as many of us were
trying to find some place to sack out up there. Even at
midnight, the ship was like a furnace down below. The fantail
was the only place I could get comfortable. I don't remember

that night as being any different from any other. All of a sudden I felt the whole ship shudder, but I still didn't know what happened. I remember shipmates telling us to stay with her, she'll be all right." Then I heard everyone tell us to "abandon ship!" There were a lot of people running around everywhere. It was mass confusion. I just did what lots of other guys did, I walked down the port side of the ship, slid down between the propeller shaft and the ship's bottom and found myself in the water."

It seemed to O'Donnell that "parts of the Philippine Sea were on fire when he first slid into it. Lots of guys were badly burned. Many were blinded or severely injured when the ship exploded, and all that fuel just spilled out of the hull into the water. I had never seen any body of water burn like that before. It was an unbelievable sight." O'Donnell suffered only minor burns. (The ship carried aviation gasoline for the scout airplanes aboard and this is what could have been burning. The black bunker oil from the ship floated out on the surface but didn't seem to catch fire. This was a blessing in that it helped to protect the men from losing body heat, and protect them from the hot sun rays that reflected on the water. The disadvantages was that it caused vomiting and nausea and the loss of fluids.)

Once in the water, O'Donnell could do no more than listen to the sound of injured shipmates dying and watch in disbelief as pieces of the once great ship floated by covered in oil. O'Donnell had presence of mind to grab a life jacket before he entered the water. When dawn broke about five hours later, he quickly discovered he was not alone floating in the debris. I never thought much about sharks until I felt one bump against my feet as they dangled in the water. There was not much I could do about those sharks as the life jacket forced you upright in the water and you could pull your legs up only so far. O'Donnell said he felt quite optimistic about rescue because he knew the USS Idaho was expecting to

143

rendezvous with the USS Indianapolis that very same day. The men reassured themselves that the Indy would be missed and a rescue mission would be mounted promptly. The first day passed with no help in sight. Only the sharks came calling. With no food, or water and the taste of fuel oil in his mouth, O'Donnell survived and hung on until help finally came. Surface currents began to spread the men over a wide area. The fact that the propellers of the USS Indy were still churning as small groups of men abandoned ship together, caused gaps between the survivors. O'Donnell said his group was about two dozen men and it didn't matter if you knew each other; it was more important to stay together for physical and emotional reasons. One could get a few moments of sleep while a buddy watched and then you could watch while he dozed off.

The sharks seemed to go after those who drifted off alone. When one would come around we would start kicking and punching the water for all we were worth. There were always hundreds of sharks swimming and bumping into your feet. You were constantly scared to death that you might be the next one they would go after.

The group was picked up about 4:00 am Friday morning by the USS Bassett but O'Donnell believes Wednesday was the breaking point for many of his comrades. Exhausted, consumed with hunger and thirst, hands and legs covered with salt water ulcers, and hallucinating, the men would swim off to an imagined "Paradise Island" just a few yards away. "I saw guys slip out of the life jackets and tell us they were going over to the hotel there, pointing to it as they swam away. Some just took off their life jackets and sank. It just got too tough and I guess they gave up. Now also the men began to fight among themselves accusing one another of stealing the water or food. Some thought a shipmate looked like a "Jap" and would attack him expending energy that should be saved. Nearly as bad as the hallucinations were the US planes flying over us. Every time we would hear or see one we would expend our energy waving, hollering and splashing the water. But the damned things would never drop down to give us a look."

"I can still see it like it was yesterday, sailors jumping from the Bassett' s LCVPs into the water to save us. The guys in the water would put you on their shoulders and push you up to the guys in the boats. At the Bassett they lowered a cargo net off the side of the ship and the Bassett's crew would jump into the water and again you got pushed aboard." Jim O'Donnell went on to say, "I can't begin to find words to describe how it finally felt to be out of that living hell!" Jim says he has been swimming only one time in the last 50 years, then he adds, " I have had my turn! "

"I can remember glancing at my skin and thinking it was going to peel right off. We all had the most God awful looking ulcers you could imagine. I was so weak. Two sailors on the Bassett were holding me up and I told them that I was okay. They let go of me and I passed out and fell flat on my face. If there is one thing I learned from that experience and I learned it the hard way, it is this: Never Give up!!!"

Day One
Mon. 30 Jul.

Day Two
Tues. 31 Jul.

Day Three
Wed. 1 Aug.

Day Four
Thur. 2 Aug.

Day Five
Fri. 3 Aug.
USS Bassett
Arrives

As the kapok life jackets become waterlogged ----------

Gerald Poor USS Indy Survivor   Fall of 1998

Gerald telephoned me from his home and had this to relate:

After he was picked up and out of the water he was put on the floor of the LCVP and went sound asleep. When a Bassett crew member came aboard to help get them up on the ship he heard the working crew say; " This one is dead, and so is this one over here." He roused himself up to let them know he hadn't given up yet. He said he knew his life jacket had about all the buoyancy gone and he was beginning to resign himself because he was so tired. When aboard the ship he remembers the Bassett crew members cutting off his clothes. He wished they wouldn't do that because he liked the uniform. Besides they were all new clothes as he was fresh out of Great Lakes Boot Camp. His shoes were like new also. He was a "country boy" and did not believe in destroying good clothes. When on board he was hungry and thirsty. Every time they came by he would ask for water. They gave him lemonade, coffee with sugar which he didn't like because of the sugar. But he wanted water-water-water and more water.

He was kept in the Samar hospital for 2-3 weeks and then was flown to Guam. He was 17 when he came into the Navy and he had about twelve days on a ship and about five days in the water before he saw land again.

Earl Riggins- Marine   Fall 1998
Indy Survivor writes:

Dear Mr Wren:

There were 7 or 8 of us in the rubber raft that a plane had dropped that afternoon. It was after midnight when the Bassett arrived and began to rescue the survivors. When the LCVP pulled up along side of the Bassett the crew on deck told us to remove our life jackets and come aboard.

(The jackets coming aboard were spreading oil all over the working deck and making it hard to stand up with the roll of the ship. The jackets were a mess and of no value because of their water saturated condition.) I told them I would not take mine off until I was firmly standing on the deck of the ship. After trying to do it my way I had to give in and let them cut the jacket off. After getting aboard I tried to sit down and rest a bit but someone told me to get into the shower. Next thing I knew was that someone was trying to wake me up as I was just sitting there wasting all the fresh water.

A lot of the survivors were fighting anything and anybody. They were still hallucinating. Survivors who were still fighting those trying to help them were put back into the bunks and given water and juice to bring them around to reality. Those who were in a poorer physical condition were easier to handle and the oil and sores could be cleaned up before they were put into the bunk. Riggans never did get all the bunker oil off his body. They removed him from the shower and put him in a bunk so he could continue to sleep.

The next morning, he said, "I went to breakfast in the mess hall and they gave me an orange. Nothing has ever tasted so good. I often wonder how they got all that grease and oil cleaned up."

Note: I met Riggins at the 1997 reunion and with his six foot plus height and trim body frame, he is still all Marine.

147

I can see why the Bassett crew decided "okay", just let him sleep for now.

A Patriot Speaks

These letters were saved to be the last item in this book because they speak to the children of today, to help them understand, that love of country, duty and honor are the greatest tributes we can give back to America and our families. Many patriots have gone before us protecting and defending the American concept of freedom. Some have just simply served when called on and have no great heroics to report. Others have been in the thick of the forays and returned home to enjoy the peace for which they fought. Still others were left on the fields and waters of war, while we the survivors, live to enjoy what they fought and bled for. We can never forget those patriots. That is why you will find us on patriotic holidays taking time to set a few hours free to say our profound thank you for their sacrifice. Mr Twible's letter shows the continuation of that spirit that lives today in the hearts of true patriots who could be your next door neighbor. On the next patriotic holiday, be it the 4th of July, Memorial Day, Pearl Harbor Day, or Veterans Day take a moment to remember that this is a gift to you because someone before you knew the value of freedom.

L. Peter Wren

28 January 1998

Ltr from Harlan M Twible

Dear Peter:

I decided I should write a book that would tell my children just what made this nation great. It wasn't those who hated this nation or refused to defend it. It was those who loved freedom and defended it. Being the son of an immigrant, I was never allowed to forget how fortunate I was to be born here. My father ensured that. Though almost illiterate, my dad had personal knowledge of what freedom in this land of plenty should mean to those living here. I tried to put this into my book. I also tried to show how important it is for a nation to act as one and protect itself from enemies without and within. My book would not have been complete without my experience on the USS Indianapolis.

Because of your request about my recollections that I might have about the rescue by the USS Bassett and the treatment we received I am enclosing pages out of my book that do mention the Bassett and the treatment we received. The enclosures are out of context if read together but make sense if read separately.

I want to commend you for your efforts in bringing the Bassett crew to the place in history that it belongs.

Sincerely yours,

/s/ Harlan M. Twible

XIV
Homeward Bound

If it had been planned in advance, a better ship for the rescue mission couldn't have been found other than the USS Bassett. It was a destroyer transport and easily accommodated the 151 men it had plucked from the sea. Its crew was used to taking on extra people and showed their skills as they gently put us down in their bunks. I was paralyzed from my waist down so I couldn't have maneuvered for myself. Within minutes, a crewman was at my side giving me sips of water. As good as the water tasted, it could not keep me from falling asleep. My five days without sleep had caught up with me. My duty was done. Others were now taking care of my crew. Now I could rest.

I felt a light tug on my oil soaked uniform. A navy corpsman and a doctor were at my side. The doctor said, "You're bleeding some place. Mind if we take a look?" Without waiting for an answer the corpsman started cutting off my clothes. At another time I would have protested. I had to buy my uniforms and waste was not my bag. This time, however, I was happy to have the attention. Finally, the doctor said, "Clean him up, lets dress his wound." He turned to me. "You were lucky. It went in the front and came out the back. They will look at you when we get to Samar. In the meantime we are going to give you a blood transfusion." I said thanks and went back to sleep.

When I awakened again, the corpsman standing nearby and came over to see if I wanted anything. The transfusion was almost completed. I wanted something to drink and I told him that I would like to get the oil out of my hair and wash all the crud off of me. He told me he had better give me a hand. I was covered with salt water ulcers. It would be better to not wash off the scabs because that could lead to more infection. He suggested that I take off my rings, watch and take my wallet out of my pocket. I had an oil-soaked twenty dollar bill, a picture of my new bride, and a membership card for the officers club in Washington. They would be safe beside my bunk. I did as he suggested. He removed the transfusion needle from my arm. I tried to get up. I didn't quite make it. My legs didn't seem to want to work. The corpsman pulled me up and took me off to my first shower in six days.

Showering was a long drawn out process, but it felt great. The corpsman gently washed between the ulcers and around the wound on my left side, There wasn't much he could do for the puss under my fingernails, the swollen fingers and hands, or the beard and sores on my face. He decided those parts would be better left for another time. He dried me and led me back to my bunk where there were clean underwear and socks for me.

As soon as I was dressed, I returned to my bunk for more sleep. Sometime later, I decided to venture out of the bunk room. I was discovering a new world. Everyone showed great deference to me as I walked about semi-clothed. I will never forget a chief petty officer coming up to me saying, "You look hungry. Come on down to the chief's mess and get something to eat." Rank had been lost on this cruise. He saw a person who had been through the mill and needed food. He wanted to get that food from his mess. I felt honored, for the chief's mess is sacrosanct and never entered by anyone but a chief. This is one time it was opened to a sailor who looked like he needed food.

Finally, Samar. Many of us were now ambulatory even if pretty well banged up. As I walked down the gangplank, I thought I was seeing a mirage. The captain who runs Misery Hall at the Academy was standing there to look over his newest patients. I introduced myself to him and his only words were, "You got here the tough way. I will be over to see you as soon as you are settled."

151

We were taken by bus and ambulance to the hospital. It was really a barracks with nurses, corpsmen and doctors running around. It was surrounded by guards. We were being held incommunicado. The bomb that we had carried to Tinian had not yet been dropped on Hiroshima so secrecy was a must. The military did not want anyone to know that we had been sunk or what we had carried. Of course, they were extra cautious. No one on our ship knew what we had on board so they couldn't have told anyone if they had wanted to.

Redmayne and I shared a room. Dick was pretty much out of his trauma and was starting to talk a blue streak. I hadn't known him very well on board ship. He was an engineer, and I was gunnery. He was known for his rough treatment of sailors and using his rank whenever he could. He was only a lieutenant at that time but was either up for, or had been chosen for, elevation to lieutenant commander. We carried on a lot of idle talk that first day. I learned he had been trained on the Massachusetts Nautical Ship, the same one on which my childhood friend, Stuart Morrison, had trained. He more or less resented Academy men. I believe that he resented the fact that I had gone there.

At one point, Dick said, "Some son of a bitch of an enlisted man gave me a hell of a crack on my head. Look at this bump."

Should I tell him or not? I decided to tell him the whole story. About his losing touch with reality. About my using morphine on him. About his deciding on the last day that he would dive down to the engine room to start the engines. (Note: It is customary for the engineering department to light off the boilers several hours before getting underway. It is customary to test the main engines an hour before getting underway so that all systems are on line and ready to go when the captain rings up the first engine order on the Engine Order Telegraph.) Redmayne is hallucinating and must be stopped. If he dives down he will

152

never return. Twible continues. At that point, I cleared the decks. "Dick you had become unmanageable. None of us had any strength. I wanted to do what I could to save you. The only thing that I could do was to knock you out. As if by an act of God a hard tack can had floated up to me. I cracked you on the head, knocked you out and then hung on to you. "

The second part of Twible's enclosure is given here.

The pilot and crew were witnessing a shark attack. They were willing to risk their lives so that we might live. Could we hold our crew together while the rescuers came to get us? This proved to be one of the toughest times, trying to keep this group together with help in sight. One Ensign decided that he couldn't wait any longer and started to swim to the plane. Everyone was too weak to stop him, and he was too weak to make the trip. He had thrown off his life jacket and swam without it. A hundred or so yards out he faltered and went under. We never saw him again. This sight helped quell the ardor of others to do the same. Again, the crew was reminded that it wouldn't be long before we were rescued. Anyone who left the group would be court-martialed when we got ashore. (I knew that anyone who left the group would never get ashore. While I never had any intention of carrying out this threat on these fabulous men, I needed something to stop them from throwing away their lives. This did it.)

Soon another plane hovered over us and more material was dropped by parachute. I turned Redmayne over to someone and told him to watch the Lieutenant. I swam to the boat that was dropped and was joined by Gunner Horner. We searched for communication equipment. We soon found a walkie talkie. Unfortunately it did not work. However, the next best thing came into sight was a mirror. Back in my old days at the Academy we were trained on this. I soon flashed out the message, "Help-We are from CA 35." The message came back: "Slow down. Identify yourself," I did. Help was on its way. We then proceeded to load the most seriously wounded into the boat. We assembled the "salt water teats" and gave each man his first swallow of water in almost five days. We lit cigarettes that were in the rescue kit and gave each man who wanted one a lit cigarette. The gunner and I kept moving around the net and telling everyone to keep calm. Help was on its way. When the Bassett came into sight, I realized that our being saved was a miracle. I looked out on this crew and couldn't believe that we were so many after such an ordeal. Yet, we were. Unfortunately, we had lost a lot of shipmates and friends, but many had survived.

Some of the crew of the Bassett towed our boat to the ship. I hung onto the stern of that boat for dear life. Two sailors tried to lift me out of the water but couldn't. My life jacket was too heavy. They did the next best thing. They cut my life jacket straps, lifted me out of it, and hoisted me up to the quarter deck. In the best Naval fashion, I reported to the Officer of the Deck, "This is the crew of the USS Indianapolis, Sir," and I was carried away.

The nightmare was over. Sleeplessness, thirst, hunger, sharks and death were gone and now rest. Now I know what the Navy Hymn means when we plead:

"0, hear us when we cry to Thee
For those in peril on the sea."

EPILOGUE

God had seen us through!

The Navy awarded me a Navy and Marine Corps Medal for bravery (Warrant Officer Gunner Horner had recommended me for it). I also received a Purple Heart for being wounded in action. But none of these things told any of the story. They couldn't. Words could never tell the story of the courage and bravery of that crew and its captain or the intrigue in the Navy bureaucracy in covering up the CNO admirals. This was a story that could never be captured and put on paper. One had to live it.

The Indianapolis' misadventure left an indelible impression on me. What decision would I ever make that would compare with my decision to ask those men to follow me into the water? Every decision since that fateful night of July 30, 1945 has been small in comparison. All would forever be.

Many other things were to carry over into my life from that experience. Fear, as, most people know it, disappeared from my makeup. No doubt it is still somewhere but of things that are not mundane. I still have an unrequited love for our country. This would never change. My lifelong disdain for and distrust of bureaucracy had its beginning in the mistakes that led to the needless loss of life. My distrust of people who could not admit to their mistakes and who heaped blame on others also probably goes back to the way the Navy treated our Captain. This shoddy treatment made me wary of anyone who made excuses and who blamed his problems on others. Most important, our experience never made me think that my country owed me anything. Bitterness did not linger.

/s/Harlan M. Twible

Chapter Five

Oral histories and letters from those who rendered medical assistance, and from family members who waited anxiously for news. A description of the thorough search of the sea by the ships present to be sure every possible survivor was recovered. Also included are the oral histories of the airplane crews who discovered the tragedy, and poems of rememberance.

SEARCH PLANS

At the rescue scene, the USS Madison DD423 acting as SOPA --Senior Officer Present Afloat-- instituted three search plans to be sure that no Indianapolis crewman was left on the open sea. In addition to this, all sinkable debris was sunken and all recoverable objects were picked up so that any aircraft or surface vessel would not continue to report sightings on this sea and thereby divert other vessels to a scene that had already been swept. An illustration of the "Search" is shown herewith.

CLOSED BOX

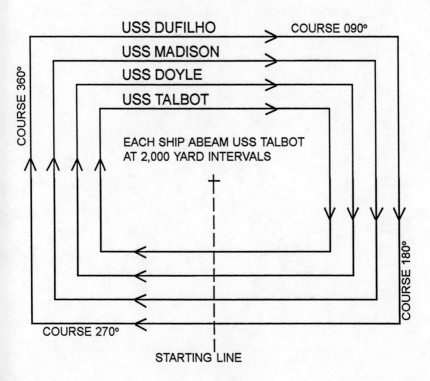

157

THE SWEEP

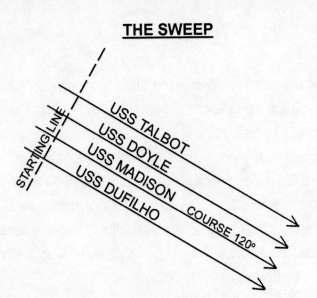

OPEN BOX

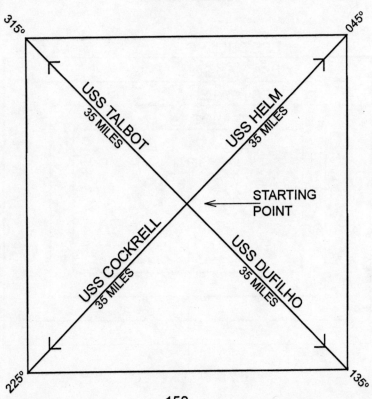

The Search

CDR Todd, the captain of the USS Madison upon arriving on the scene was able to transfer his ship's doctor, Lt Harlan A Stiles to the Bassett's fantail by boatswain chair as was observed by Ensign Wren of the Bassett. With Doctor Stiles aboard and at about 6:00 am the Bassett departed for Samar Island P.I. The Bassett was under the Philippine Sea Frontier Command {PSF} and as this was the command that had issued the orders to search for the survivors, it was logical, that the ship return to the Samar Medical Facility of PSF. The Samar Medical facility was just getting set up prior to the planned invasion of Japan scheduled for November 1945. The Facility had hospital beds for 3000 with 26 doctors and 101 nurses preparing for the casualties that could result from the planned invasion of Kyushu Island of Japan. At 8:00 am Saturday 4 August, 1945 with Ensign L. Peter Wren at the conn, the USS Bassett sailed into the harbor of Guinian on Samar Island, P.I. From Wren's observation the line of Red Cross ambulances waiting to transport the survivors seemed endless.

The USS Doyle, skippered by LCDR Graham Claytor, had transferred 56 survivors from Lt Mark's PBY airplane which was now drifting on the sea. The Doyle also recovered 37 more survivors making their on board total 93. This was the second largest group recovered. The 56 on the wings and in the fuselage of the PBY were not in as bad of shape as those picked up by the Bassett. It took the Doyle about several hours to transfer the 56 men by motor whaleboat. By dawn the Doyle's boats had completed the last trip to Mark's plane After the removal of the salvage gear and the crew from the PBY the Doyle trained its guns on the PBY sinking the floating hull which had become an island of relief from the sun, the sea and the sharks. The Doyle, at 12 noon, with permission from SOPA, CDR Todd, left for Peleliu. The

Bassett had already left before 6:00am that same morning. This made it difficult for the SOPA to report the full number recovered. The Bassett reported to Adm. Kinkaid of the PSF, while Captain Todd [SOPA] reported to Adm. Nimitz, CINCPAC Guam.

The USS Madison DD 425 arrived at the scene of the Indy's sinking at approximately 0400 hours on Friday the 3rd of August 1945 and quickly placed Ltjg Harlan Stiles, Medical Corps, USNR on the fantail of the USS Bassett. The Bassett by this time had just about a full load of the USS Indy survivors on board. Most were stretcher cases and Dr. Royce Pruet on the Bassett was hard pressed to care for the 152 men in critical condition. Even with the help of two doctors, two pharmacist mates and the off duty ship's crew there was still a great need for professional help.

The USS Register with 38 survivors, and the USS Ringness with 39 survivors left for Peleliu at 4:15pm. The USS Madison [SOPA] instituted a search plan with the remaining vessels and the newly arrived ships to thoroughly search the sea area. In reading the USS Madison's log book, a sketch (enclosed) will make it easier to understand, rather than to describe it verbally. USS Indy spilled the men over a wide area as was reported by Lt. Gwinn. The USS Doyle after placing her survivor group in the Medical Facility at Peleliu was told to return to the area of the sinking to continue the search.

The search continued in the area by the USS Madison DD 425, the USS Talbot DE 390 and the USS Dufilho DE 423 for the rest of Friday the 3rd of August 1945. By dawn on Saturday the USS Aylwin DE 355, the USS Helm DE 388 arrived and were incorporated into the search plans. A little later the USS Cockrell DE 225 and the USS French were able to add their presence to the search plans. According to the USS Madison's log the search was conducted by three different search plans as I understood them. Namely, the Box, the Sweep and the Extended Box. In the process four bodies were recovered, identified, and buried at sea.

The handling of these men or their bodies if they have died, is very difficult task. To try to pull them out of the water after five days of exposure their flesh is very soft and easily pulls away from the bone structure. It was said on one of the ships, as crew watched shipmates help haul the men aboard, that many just stood there and cried. The most merciful way to bring them from the LCVP's or the whaleboats was to use the wire baskets.

The search also included the recovery of unsinkable gear as well as sinking every item that was sinkable. It was necessary to rid the sea of this debris, otherwise ships and aircraft passing through the area would be reporting and overloading the radio circuits already carrying heavy loads of radio traffic. The search and clean up continued until Tuesday August 7, 1945 when the USS Madison [SOPA] released all the ships feeling everything that could be done was accomplished.

A report on the arrival times and the number of men recovered is listed herewith.

Ship Name		Arrival Time	Rescued
USS DOYLE DE 368	Fri 3 Aug'45	0015	93
USS BASSETT APD 73	Fri 3 Aug'45	0052	152
USS REGISTER APD 92	Fri 3 Aug'45	0200	12
USS DUFILHO DE 423	Fri 3 Aug'45	0300	1
USS MADISON DD 425	Fri 3 Aug'45	0400	-0-
USS TALBOT DE 390	Fri 3 Aug 45	0500	24
USS RINGNESS APD 100	Fri 3 Aug'45	1025	39

Note: The survivors from the Dufilho and the Talbot were transferred to the Register. The Register then proceeded to

Peleliu relieving these two ships to continue the search for survivors who could still be adrift. Although 321 were picked up by the rescue ships, four later died making the living total 317. Other Ships that aided in the rescue and search: USS Aylwin, USS Cockrell, USS Helm, and USS French.

Ltr from Herbert Hickman
Gwinn's Crew   September 1998

Herbert Hickman sent me a copy of the speech he was prepared to deliver at the Dedication of the USS Indianapolis Monument for my use. Hickman was an aviation ordinance man and turret gunner on Lt Gwinn's Ventura VBP-152. Later I corresponded with his wife and she sent me the same material that was sent previously by Herbert. Given below is the speech that was never delivered at the USS Indianapolis Monument Dedication Ceremony and Reunion held in Indianapolis, Indiana on August 2, 1995 because of the time restraints of that days events.

The Six Most Important Words of Your Life

As I stand before you now, and think back to that day of miracles, August 2nd 1945, 1 remember all the things that happened. I know and understand that God was answering many prayers at that moment of our lives. God answered those prayers and Lt Chuck Gwinn and his crew were there as things happened that made us unknowingly progress to the point that your rescue started.

On that day we were assigned the task of checking out a new type of trailing weight for our long range communication radio system. Lt. Gwinn took the aircraft off, the antenna was reeled out and the new weight separated in about two minutes. We returned to base and another one was

162

installed. This time Lt Gwinn took the aircraft off but waited until we were well on our way toward your position in the Pacific when the antenna wire was reeled out for the second time. It remained intact for about five minutes when our radioman, Chief Bill Hartman, reported to Lt. Gwinn that the second weight had broke off from the antenna wire and our long range communication was now inoperative. Joseph K. Johnson and I were given the task of trying to retrieve the antenna wire through a window in the bottom of the aircraft, and to find something to attach to it to make it trail our aircraft. The antenna was whipping around viciously, and we were trying to devise an extension of some kind to reach it. Lt. Gwinn turned the flight of the aircraft over to the co-pilot, Lt. Colwell, and he came back to try to help.

All this time we had progressed on our assigned patrol heading to a point almost due west of your position and approximately fifteen nautical miles from you. This would be 356 nautical miles from our base on Peleliu. Lt. Gwinn, your "Angel", came back and knelt down at the tunnel window to look at the situation. While doing so, he suddenly jumped up and headed for the front of the aircraft. I shouted to him above the noise of the aircraft "What was the matter?" And he said, " LOOK DOWN AND YOU WILL SEE!" At that moment your rescue started. I looked down, for what seemed to be a long time but I imagine it was around 20 seconds before the wave's position reflected the suns rays up to me. At that instant it revealed the oil slick, and then it was gone from view. I seriously doubt that J.K. Johnson or I would have noticed the oil slick because our minds and attention were directed on the antenna. At this moment we thought we had a Japanese sub, and we were at that instant on a search and destroy mission. As we circled down and watched the oil slick at a very low altitude for approximately fifteen nautical miles, and at as fast a speed as our aircraft could attain, we came upon you and all the debris. I cannot

163

describe to you the astonishment that we felt at that moment. And to this day as I think back on the scene, I am continuously amazed in that split second we were transformed from a search and destroy mode to a concerned and compassionate rescue team circling over you. So in closing I would like to say, remember those six words which are the most important to your life today, said by your "angel" Wilbur C. "Chuck" Gwinn.

"LOOK DOWN AND YOU WELL SEE"

Hickman continued in his letter--

When we saw the oil slick we thought we had a Japanese sub snorkeling on the surface and recharging his batteries just east of our assigned course. When we came across the survivors and all the debris on the surface of the ocean, radio silence was broken immediately with an urgent message for any surface vessel or aircraft to come and render aid to the men in the shark infested waters.

/s/ Herbert Hickman

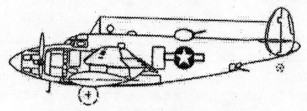

August 2. A Navy PV-1 Ventura spotted debris and survivors over a 20 mile area.

Joseph K. Johnson,   5 January 1999
Airplane crew

Dear LCDR Wren:

In answer to your request for information on my part in the rescue of the survivors of the USS Indianapolis, I am pleased to relate the following: The below enlisted men and officers were the flight crew of a PV-I Ventura Bomber # 538 which was one of fifteen aircraft of the USNavy VPB- 152 Squadron.

LT Wilber Charles Gwinn	Pilot
LT. Warren G. Coldwell	Co Pilot
Chief Win [Bill] Hartmen	CRdM
Herbert [Herb] Hickman	AOM3/c
Joseph K. Johnson	AMM1/c

I, Joseph K. Johnson, am the only surviving member of this air crew.

On 2 August 1945, the above were flying an assigned sector to search and destroy any Japanese submarines they might find in their flight sector. The mission was completed and they were enroute to their air base on the Island of Peleliu. About half way back to the base LT Gwinn decided to try out a new trailing aerial antenna which had just been installed on the aircraft. Herbert Hickman let out the aerial to trail behind the aircraft but it whipped around so much that the weight on the outer end broke off. LT Gwinn was not going to give up, so after winding the aerial in, I came up with a piece of rubber hose which he attached to the very end. I don't know whether it worked or not because very shortly after it was paid out, LT Gwinn saw an oil slick below on the water's surface and called to both Hickman and me to verify his sighting. We, of course, saw it and we, like LT Gwinn thought we had a Japanese submarine below in the water. As we opened the bomb bay doors and were ready to drop our bombs when the altitude was about 500 feet, we began to see the yellow life vests in the water. As we flew as low as possible without blowing the swimmers out of the water with our propeller wash, we became aware that there were a lot of men down there, either Japanese or Americans. At this time we threw all the safety gear we had down to them. One of the things was a radio [waterproof] which could send and receive messages. Someone in the water evidently knew what to do with it and advised us that they were Americans and that they were from the USS Indianapolis.

Our radioman Bill Hartman sent out messages to Peleliu and to all the surrounding ships in the area. We continued to circle around the area until our captain from Peleliu, LCDR Atleberry, flew out to relieve us before we ran out of gasoline. That is my story inasmuch as we enlisted men were not allowed to go see the survivors who had been taken to Peleliu for hospitalization. Each of us was awarded the "Air Medal" for our part in the rescue.

/s/ Joseph K. Johnson.

Samar Medical Facility

The Richmond Times Dispatch interviewed L. Peter Wren on July 25, 1979 regarding his personal experience in the rescue of the survivors of the USS Indianapolis. Wren was a boat officer from the USS Bassett [APD 73] which was sent to investigate "unknown objects in the Philippine Sea." Working out of a rescue boat Wren was pulling survivors from the USS Indianapolis out of the shark infested water. The article was quite lengthy and gave some of the sordid details of that night. Three or four days before the same paper had an article on a survivor from the Roanoke area named Belcher who was rescued by another ship. As a result of the article, Mr. Stan Nelson, an employee of the A.H. Robins

Company here in Richmond, Va. dropped Wren the following note.

Sept 5,1979

Dear Mr. Wren

I very much appreciate the Bassett story that you sent me. I very well remember the Bassett coming to Samar with a good number of survivors, many close to death. At the time no one wanted to admit that the Indianapolis had been sunk by the Japanese. I also remember a number of our doctors being very upset that they were forced via orders from Guam to send many of the injured there for interrogation. Some were not fit for air travel. Our Senior Medical Officer objected, but was overruled. A number of the survivors died at Guam.

It seems like such a long time ago, but many of my experiences still flash back to me from time to time. I was a Pharmacist mate first class at that time. My tour of duty started in the Russell Islands, from there to Bouganville, to Ouvi and Biak in the Dutch Schoten Islands, then to the small villages of Guiana on the Island of Samar where I attended the survivors. Thank you for sharing your experience with me.

Sincerely,
Stan Nelson

Ltr from William E. Sprague, MD 21 December 1998

Dear CDR Wren:

I believe it was 4 August 1945 while stationed at Base Hospital #20 on Peleliu Island that a rumor was afloat about some survivors of a ship sinking were coming to our hospital. I was a Hospital Apprentice 1st class, having been assigned there after my detachment from the First Marine Division following the Peleliu Invasion. The First Marines went on to Okinawa.

167

I was doing duty at the hospital when all these sailors came in, blackened with oil. Many were still delirious and babbling about sharks, completely exhausted. All of them had extensive inflammation of their eyes and the majority had severe sunburns with peeling skin and parched lips. One of the first things we wanted to do was to start intravenous fluids for their obvious dehydration. We ran into a real problem in attempting to do this because their skin was so seared it was extremely difficult to find a vein in which we could insert a needle. I remember in one case we had to use the dorsal vein of the penis.

Following the rehydration and some liquid nutrition for a few days these survivors began to improve quite rapidly, especially mentally. I am not sure how many survivors we had but it must have been sixty or seventy. Maybe more, perhaps less. I know that Captain McVay was there and he seemed to be in better shape than any of his shipmates. He was always walking around with his captains hat on talking with the doctors and to the survivors. I never met him or talked with him.

The word got around very rapidly that these were men from the USS Indianapolis and had been on the receiving end of three Japanese torpedoes. I would hear the tales of ninety hours in the ocean before being found; the ever presence of sharks; of being attacked by them and of shipmates being pulled under; of screaming at the tops of their voices; of holding hands and praying; of shipmates delusions and breaking loose saying they wanted to go "below decks" for a drink of water; and never to be seen again; of separation from other groups of sailors and feeling lonely and wondering if they would ever be found; of torrid daylight sun and the stillness in the water as darkness arrived.

In more somber moments they talked about not being on a zigzag course. They also said this happened around midnight and I am quite positive they said that the smoking

168

lamp was lit. They also said that after the torpedoes hit it wasn't very long until they had to abandon ship. A couple of them mentioned that some of their shipmates below the main deck never made it topside and the water was gushing everywhere below the main deck.

I don't recall from what port they had left but I seem to recall they were heading for the Philippine Islands. Nothing was ever mentioned to me about Tinian or the atomic bomb. I think they were still on Peleliu when the atomic bomb was dropped on Hiroshima and were all stunned and wondered what it meant to us. We assumed that with the impending invasion of Japan we would all be involved and were concerned with the uncertainty of our own lives in the future. If I recollect correctly the survivors were at our Base Hospital for approximately two weeks and then transferred to Honolulu.

More importantly for me though was from my medical experience as a medical corpsman with the 1st Marines and the duties from New Caledonia, Guadacanal, Russell Islands, the invasion of Peleliu and the subsequent experience in caring for the survivors of the USS Indianapolis. I discovered the sadness of war, the wanton destruction of human lives of ourselves and of our enemies. I became involved as a volunteer in international health, primarily in developing countries. This I have done once or twice a year and continue to do so since 1962. The experience of international conflict in the early years of my life gave me profound direction in the courses of which my life would take.

Sincerely
William E. Sprague, MD

Ltr from Robert H. Belding PhM 2/c   14 Jan 1999
USS Tranquillity AH11

Dear Mr. L. Peter Wren:

Our Hospital Ship, the Tranquillity, was based in the Ulithi Islands when not in action. I was the senior corpsman for two wards with a doctor and three nurses. One day we got underway without my knowing where we were going. We dropped anchor near Peleliu in the Palau Islands. The next day we were notified to prepare for a lot of patients. Soon, another ship came along side of ours and started to unload their patients to our ship. The thirty patients who were assigned to my wards were given blood plasma intravenously immediately. I was told that they had been in the water for five days. One man had a reaction to the blood plasma and was taken off the IV because of violent body shaking.

The Doctor and I interviewed each man for his history record. I was told of the horrible times they had with the sharks, fights over the hats that some men had while others were hatless. Fights were over the fact that there was not enough room for each man in a raft or lifeboat. They were to trade places periodically but did not do so peacefully. There were salt water sores in all cavities of their bodies. They were sun burned very badly. During the interviews they would relate what transpired during the five days spent in the water. They would watch their fellow shipmates just give up and float away and die. Upon receiving all the men from the other ship, we got underway for the Naval Hospital in Guam. I will never forget that experience.

Sincerely
/s/Robert H. Belding PhM2/c USNR

Mary Alice O'Donnell
Survivor's wife
Oral Interview July 1997 and parts of the
News Article Harrison Post 27 July 1995 by C. Calkins

Mary Alice O'Donnell was the two year bride of Jim O'Donnell, a sailor on the USS Indy, who received a telegram on 14 August 1945 telling her that her husband "James was a victim of water immersion." She didn't know exactly what that meant. She wondered if he was a victim of a boiler room accident or what? She wondered if she was a war widow only after two years of married life. She knew her "Jim" was on a ship but she didn't know where the ship was in the Pacific Ocean. It was on the next day August 15th that the local newspaper in Indianapolis announced that the USS Indianapolis was sunk after carrying the atomic bomb parts to Tinian Island. The headline read **"PEACE-WAR IS ENDED."** Then there followed a smaller article stating, **"Nip Sub Sinks Cruiser Indianapolis."**

The Newspaper goes on to report the fact that the Indianapolis had carried the bomb and that 883 of the crew were lost. Alice ODonnell said: "The head lines first, and now the article. It just floored me." She continues, "I was devastated. I wasn't sure how many men Jim's ship carried, but I knew that 883 was a large percentage of them. Well one shoe had dropped with news about the immersion, when would the second shoe drop."

After two weeks of agony, Mary Alice received a Navy letter saying that "James was alive and on the Island of Samar, from which he would be transported to the Island of Guam and that he was expected to make full recovery."

Today the messages are under glass in her Indianapolis home and reminds them of how things were in those war years. Alice said, "Today with TV, the families of military men can sit in their living rooms and watch the ensuing battles that their loved ones are facing. News is instant and the anxiety may be of a much shorter duration."

GRIEVING

July 1997 Reunion

Bereaved persons need to talk about their losses, since grief sharing is grief diminished. Each time a griever talks about the loss, a layer of grief is shed. The loss of a loved one at sea leaves the bereaved without a place to release his burden. Loved ones lost on a trackless sea need that monument where family can go and say their personal good bye and know that the loved one is at rest within the confines of that Monument. Here they find friends with understanding hearts, a sympathetic ears, and a final resting place so they can start their life anew.

Having written that, let me tell you about a bereaved sister whose brother was lost with the sinking of the Indianapolis. Her brother was a storekeeper who would have had his 21st birthday on July 31st. His sister and I met on the bus leaving from the Monument at the 1997 reunion. She was in a wheel chair and came from her home town to see if she could meet someone who knew her brother.

We had difficulty getting the special loading ramp working, and I helped her on the bus as the driver got the ramp in the right position. I wheeled her into a proper place for wheel chairs on the bus, locked the chair's brakes and sat down in a seat next to her so I could help her off the bus. She was traveling alone and had two knee replacements recently. One knee cap was heavily scarred and she said that operation on that knee hadn't been too successful. The other knee was just fine.

She reached in her large handbag and pulled out a green covered book. She asked if I knew her brother who

172

was a storekeeper on the Indianapolis. My answer was "No, I was from one of the rescue ships. Do you know what ship rescued him.?" She stated he went down with the ship and she was looking for someone who knew him and could tell her about her brother. She opened the book and there in calendar order was a list of the people she had asked concerning her brother. She kept the list so she would have record of whom she had asked so as to avoid bothering them again. She took my name and address and placed it carefully on the dated line in her book.

Here is a woman grieving for her brother; she won't put him to rest until some one says they knew "James" and assures her he is in Gods hands. I never did get her last name and I hesitated to ask as she queried the man across the aisle. From 1945 to 1997 is 52 years of grieving. I believe his name was James H. Mitchell, SK1/c.

I wondered how many other families are experiencing similar grief associated with the Indianapolis tragedy. Reading over the ship's company that sailed out of Guam on that fateful day revealed that a large percent of the young men were just out of basic training and in their teens. This was in most cases their first ship. There really wasn't much time to get to know all the decks and different escape routes to the top side. The Indy was on a "hurry up" secret mission and perhaps the usual training of new sailors was put on hold until the special cargo was delivered. Even if you did know an alternative route there was hardly time. God grant peace for all those who went down with the ship and their families!

Coincidences

Certain events occurring around the USS Bassett make me feel the ship has an unusual history. The events have gone quietly unnoticed for years and yet I believe they should be brought forth for contemplation. The Bassett is a converted Destroyer Escort that has great "utility," namely as a fast transport in the US Navy. The Bassett won no "Battle Stars," sunk no enemy submarines, nor did she lay down a heavy bombardment on enemy installations, but she did have these interesting connections in her history.

First coincidence: The USS Arizona was the FIRST ship to be sunk at the start of WWII. One of the few surviving Officers attached to the USS Arizona was LCDR Sam Fuqua who was recipient of the Congressional Medal of Honor for his outstanding performance of duty in saving two hundred plus of the crew when the Arizona was so heavily damaged and sunk at Pearl Harbor. Our connection is the marriage of his daughter Patricia to one of the USS Bassett's Commanding Officers, namely LT Charles L. Nagle USN who later on became CO of the Bassett.

Second coincidence: The USS Bassett is named after Ensign Edgar Bassett a USNR aviator who was lost in the Battle of Midway which was the turning point of the war. The Japanese Navy lost four of their Carriers and many of their experienced aviators.

Third coincidence: The USS Bassett was one of the first ships to arrive at the scene of the sinking of the USS Indianapolis, the LAST ship to be sunk in WWII. The USS Indianapolis had just delivered the atomic parts that when used would end WWII. Of the 1197 men aboard the USS Indianapolis only 317 were rescued from the sea. The USS Bassett was able to recover 152 of the men who fought the sun, the sharks and the sea for five days.

So as the writer sees it, the Bassett was involved in some way with the FIRST and LAST events of the World War II. It was Ensign Bassett who gave his all for his country in the Battle of Midway that gave the ship its name.

Another piece of history is told by Mrs. Patricia Fuqua Nagle about her father on the night before the attack on Pearl Harbor. LCDR Fuqua had the "in port" watch and he was to be relieved by LT Kelly. LT Kelly had his wife and two daughters come aboard the evening of December 6, 1941 for dinner. It would be their last chance to be together for some time. LCDR Fuqua suggested that LT Kelly spend the evening with his family and that he would take his watch. Kelly accepted Fuqua's offer and left the ship with his family. LCDR Fuqua decided to take his rest in the space provided near the Quarterdeck rather than go below to his compartment. When the bombs rained down on Pearl Harbor that Sunday morning on December 7, 1941 Fuqua was up and leading the men in the fire fighting to save the USS Arizona. He was credited with saving over 200 men. For this action he received the Congressional Medal of Honor, which is the nation's highest award. In later days at Pearl Harbor, Fuqua donned diving gear and went below into the sunken hull of the Arizona to recover some of his personal belongings. He said his compartment was in shambles and had he gone there to spend the night he would not have made it out. His uniforms were hanging in his closet and swaying back and forth in the ocean current drifting through the ship.

Another coincidence around the war years of WWII is the dates on which the war started and ended. The Bassett has no connection with these dates but the reader is encouraged to think on them. The war was started on December 7th 1941 and was ended on the 14th of August 1945. These dates, in both incidences, are one day before the religious days cited herewith. The Immaculate Conception celebrated on December 8th of each year; and the Assumption is celebrated on August 15 of each year. These are special days in the Roman Catholic Church year when the Blessed Mother Mary is honored by prayer and recitation of the Rosary.

Further the Atomic Bomb was flown from Tinian Island which is part of the Marianas Group. These islands are believed to have been named "the Marianas" by the Spanish Jesuits in 1668, because the string of small Islands curving north from the larger Islands of Guam, Rota, Saipan and Tinian reminded them of a decade of beads on a Rosary. The Rosary is a prayer to the Blessed Mother "Mary" said on five decades of beads asking the Blessed Mother to intercede with the Lord in that person's behalf.

Congratulations

Below is the recognition the USS Bassett received. The oral histories and letters recited in this book by the survivors and their families is by far the best and only the real thank you the crew has ever received

The failure in communications, the cover up of the Indianapolis' secret mission, and the delay in Japan's accepting the terms of the surrender until after the second bomb was dropped, overshadowed the heroic work of the rescue ships. In war time years the standard brief and terse acknowledgment that was offered is shown below.

PHILIPPINE SEA FRONTIER
Phil/f3/mj
F20
Serial: 2930
RESTRICTED

From: Commander Philippine Sea Frontier
To: Commanding Officer, USS Bassett [APD 73]
Subject: Rescue of Survivors, Excellent Performance

1. The Commander of the Philippine Sea Frontier is impressed with the alertness, efficiency, and devotion to duty by all hands on the Bassett in connection with the recent rescue operations at sea. *

2. The commanding Officer is to be congratulated on this demonstration of good spirit and training which was responsible for saving of many precious lives.

/s/ N. C. Gillette
Acting

Copy to:
ComTransDiv 107
*Who would know it was the USS Indianapolis?

The Sailor's Widow

Here romantically on this beach they stand
   With barefoot toe, and hand in hand.
They vow this will be their special place
   As ocean spray christens their loving embrace.

Sad the day they learned that he must be
   That sailor who, duty calls back to the sea.
He will sail forth to another patriot's war
   And she will wait as she has done before.

He smiled and said: "Wait and be brave! "
   "For soon I will return on the breaking wave."
But now she stands on that same shore
   And this beach is not what it was before.

It has become for her a lonely place
   Where never again will she feel his embrace.
Yes, the sea gull calls and soars as before
   And the wave chases the sandpipers on the shore.

The wind whips spray upon her face and hair
   She stands and sighs and is lonely there.
Her heart is heavy and her face is wet with tear.
   She waits and looks, knowing he will never appear.

L. Peter Wren
VEPAP0651492-129

ODE TO A SAILOR
by Kenneth J. Hobin

On a sailor's grave no flowers grow
Nor stones to mark them row on row
No date to say when they did die
No spot to mark where they must lie.

On a sailor's grave no friend will come
To kneel and say: " I knew this one."
No grass will keep it cool and warm
To help him sleep beneath a storm.

On the sailor's grave it will not say
How one fine day he sailed away
To keep this nation free from strife
And in that fight, he gave his life.

On a sailor's grave there is no way
To read the reason he has gone away
A Navy telegram came, and it said:
"We regret he is missing, he is not dead."

On a sailor's grave the sea rolls on;
Once he was here and now he is gone.
But do not grieve for a man of the sea,
There is no other place he would rather be.

Excerpts from the Log of the USS Bassett (APD73)

The USS Bassett was named in honor of Ensign Edgar R. Bassett USNR who was born in Philadelphia on 10 March 1914. He entered the US Navy on 13 February 1940 at age 26 and was subsequently commissioned as an Ensign--Naval Aviator. At age 28 he was killed in action on June 4th 1942 in the Battle of Midway. The Battle of Midway was the first American victory of WWII and proved to be a turning point of the war. The USS Bassett was commissioned at Orange, Texas on 23 February 1945 and proceeded to Guantanamo Bay, Cuba for shakedown exercises which continue until the 28th of March 1945. Upon completion of the shakedown exercises the Bassett departed for Norfolk, Va. More shakedown exercises were conducted in the Chesapeake Bay under the direction of ComPhib Training Command, US Atlantic Fleet. After completion of training, and having some repair made at the Portsmouth Naval Yard the Bassett was dispatched to Guantanamo Bay 24 April 1945 from which place 65 Naval personnel were transported aboard to San Diego via the Panama Canal. The ship passed through the canal and reported on I May 1945 to the Commander in Chief US Pacific Fleet and departed for San Diego on that date. Upon arrival at San Diego on 9 May 1945 a report of readiness was made to the Commander Western Pacific Frontier for onward routing. Repairs were commenced this date at San Diego Repair Base and upon their completion on 12 May 1945 departure was made for Pearl Harbor, T.H. The ship's logs reflects the following dates:

18 May '45   Arrived in Pearl Harbor, T.H. where further repairs were made. The camouflage design was removed, training exercises continued and upon completion the Bassett was routed as follows:

9 June '45	Departed Pearl Harbor, T.H. enroute to Eniwetok Atoll, Marshall Islands.
14 June '45	Crossed the International Time Date line i.e. the 180th Meridian. Crew members of the Golden Dragon.
17 June '45	Arrived Eniwetok in company with several ships
20 June '45	Departed Eniwetok for Guam in company with two ships.
23 June '45	Arrived Apra Harbor, Guam
25 June '45	Departed Guam for Ulithi Atoll, Caroline Islands in company with two ships.
27 June '45	Arrived Ulithi Atoll
2 July '45	Reported to Commander Philippine Sea Frontier ready for duty.
8 July '45	Departed Ulithi Atoll for Hollandia, New Guinea.
9 July '45	Crossed the Equator. Held King Neptune Rex ceremonies 0 degree 00minutes and 133degrees 59minutes East.
10 July '45	Arrived Hollandia, New Guinea
13 July '45	Enroute to Leyte Island, P.I. in company of two ships.
15 July '45	While enroute to Leyte Island rescued Lt Walter L Hilgart USAAF 80th Squadron. Location South Pacific Ocean I degree North and 134 degrees 48 minutes East.
19 July '45	Arrived Leyte Island, P.I. Disembarked Lt. Hilgart.
21 July '45	Departed Leyte Island, P.I. with troops and mail for the following ports.

> Cebu City, Cebu Island, P. 1.
> Zamboanga, Mindanoa. P.I. Sulu Sea
> Brunei Bay, Borneo, South China Sea
> PuertoPrincessa, Palawan Island, P.I.

181

Iloilo, Panay Island, P.I.
Macajalar Bay, Minandao P.I.

26 July '45 Island run completed and returned to Leyte

31 July '45 Assigned to patrol north coast of Leyte Island by COMPHILSEAFRONTIER.[PSF]

2 Aug '45 Urgent dispatch received to proceed to position 11 degrees 54 minutes North and 133 degrees 47 minutes East to search for survivors of an unknown ship.

Pursuant to these orders the Bassett left the assigned patrol sector at 1500 hours[Item] and proceeded at best speed to the area named. At 0030 hours 3 August 1945 the area was reached and immediately thereafter the ships LCVP's began rescue missions. 152 survivors were rescue with two dying on board. The survivors were from the USS Indianapolis [CA 35]. An immediate report was made to the COM PSF. When other ships began to arrive at the site, the Bassett departed the area and arrived at Guinian Samar Island, P.I. at 0800 4 August 1945 where survivors were transferred to the Field Hospital at that location. The ship's log indicates an LCM came out to meet the Bassett bringing a total of 26 doctors and hospital corpsmen. Having discharged our passengers the Bassett returned to Leyte Island same date.

4 August '45 Depart Guinian Harbor, Samar for Leyte, PI

6 Aug '45 Departed Leyte enroute to Hollandia, New Guinea. While at sea learned the atomic bomb was dropped and still didn't know the part the USS Indianapolis played in the delivery of the bomb to Tinian.

15 Aug '45 Departed Hollandia convoying two ships.

21 Aug '45	Arrived Leyte Island, P.I.
1 Sept '45	Ordered to Manila, P.I.
3 Sept '45	Arrived Manila and reported to COM PHIB GRP 8 Fifth Fleet
7 Sept '45	Departed Manila for Okinawa
18 Sept'45	Arrived Buckner Bay, Okinawa assigned "picket line duty"
21 Sept'45	Made Rendezvous with LCT Flotilla 39 at Unten Ko, Okinawa from which place we acted as escort to the LCT convoy to Wakayama, Japan.
25 Sept'45	Arrived Wakayama and Nagoya. Discharged occupational troops[HECP] duties at Wakanoura Wan at Nagoya, Japan
04 Oct. '45	Departed Wakanoura wan enroute to Hirowan, Honsho acting as escort for 5 LSM's with 196 men and 12 Officers aboard. Troops aboard were detached to take the surrender of the Army post at Hirowan. {Kure}
06 Oct'45	Arrived Hirowan where troops and Officer's were put ashore.
07 Oct'45	Departed Hirowan with 5 LSM's in company and enroute to Wakayama, Japan
08 Oct'45	Arrived Wakayama, Japan. Assigned harbor entrance control post at Nagoya
11 Oct '45	Rode out a typhoon at anchor at Wakanoura Wan. 17 fathoms water with 90 fathoms of chain to starboard anchor. Let out port anchor with 45 fathoms of chain. No. 1 boiler on line. Lit off #2 boiler in case it would be needed to proceed to sea. Ship dragged 1000 fathom toward shore before typhoon ended.
28 Oct 145	HECP duty at Nagoya until 30 Oct 1945

01 Nov '45	Enroute to Sasebo, Japan
06 Nov'45	Anchored off Sasebo,
21 Nov '45	Ordered to Pearl Harbor with full load of passengers for discharge from Naval service due to point system
06 Nov'45	Arrive Pearl Harbor.
14 Dec '45	Arrive San Diego

On December 14 1945 Lt Charles Nagle became the commanding officer with Ltjg Ralph Horwitz as executive officer. On 8 December we passed through the Panama Canal and made standard speed for Philadelphia. Once we rode the waves of the Atlantic Ocean we could proudly say: "Back alive in 1945!" We had a short stay in the Philadelphia Navy Yard, and thank God we left soon because we were not used to the cold weather. We made a short stop in Norfolk where I had begun my career in the Navy as an apprentice seaman. Four and a half years later I had been promoted to Ltjg. At Green Cove Springs, Florida, Ltjg James Jackson came aboard and took on the executive officers job. James Jackson was very good in that position as morale was low in most cases as we struggled to get the ship into a mothball cocoon. I left the Bassett on 26 April 1946 for Richmond, Va. where I married my bride a year later. The USS Bassett was decommissioned on 29 April 1946.

They say it is a small world and I believe it. On December 1950 James Jackson and L. Peter Wren were recalled for the Korean War. We met again in San Diego in the uniform shop being outfitted for another tour of duty. I guess we didn't get it right the first time so the Navy was giving us a second chance.

USS Bassett Ship's Roll Call
August 1945

Officers

Harold Theriault	LCDR USNR	Commanding
Jas. W. Henderson	Lt USNR	Exec.Officer
Ralph R. Axtell	Lt. USNR	I st Lieut.
Thomas W. Evans	Lt. USNR	Gunnery
Royce W. Pruet	Lt jg USNR	Medical
Wm. T. Anderson	Lt jg USN	Engineering
Spencer E. Van Dyke	Ens. USNR	Communications
Ralph S. Horwitz	Lt jg USNR	ASW Officer
L. Peter Wren	Ens. USNR	Ass't I st Lieut
0. Russell Lindsey	Ens. USNR	Supply Officer
Arthur 0. Leweke	Ens. USNR	Asst Engineering
Norman G. DeLisle	Ens. USNR	Asst Commications
Jack Broser	Ens. USNR	Boat Officer
Malcom A. Smook	Ens. USNR	Asst Gunnery
Kenneth T. Hager	Ens. USNR	Asst Boat Officer

Chief Petty Officers

Daniel I Desmond	CEM
Marion W. Disch	CWT
T. H. Hines	CBM
Joseph 1. Morin	CCStd
Victor E. Neumayer	CPhM

Crew

Akins, j. c.	Ck2c	AlbaneseC.A.	BM1c
Anderson, A.0.	BMlc	Andrews, L.L.	S 2c
Arellano,A.	S 2c	Arms, I H.	MM3c
Arthur, J.D.	F Ic	Auch, H.J.	WT2c
Balvin, J.O.	S 2c	Bannon, R.D.	S Ic
Bargsley, IS.	RM3c	Barhill, G.H.	BM2c
Baron, H. P.	MM3c	Bash, R. W.	F Ic
BeaL, K. L.	GM3c	Bednar, R.L.	Cox
Bell, C.E.	F 2c	Berger, M.	F 2c
Berry, R, L.	F Ic	BiermeirR. C.	S Ic
Bland, M. E.	S Ic	Blankenship, M.	S Ic
Bliss, A. E.	EM2c	Boertlein, G.M.	F Ic
Booker, D. W.	S Ic	Borkowski, W.	Cox
Bosley, H. G.	GM3c	Braden, F. B.	F Ic
Brady, J. W.	S Ic	Bridges, L. D.	S 2c
Burchell, P. H.	S 2c	Burger, E. B.	S 2c
Burkett, I C.	S 2c	Burton, W. A.	Stm2c
Byrd, J.A.	S 2c	Calnon, T. L.	F Ic

185

Campbell, W.	S Ic	Carpenter, S. P,	F 2c
Cash, D. A.	S Ic	Chancer, E.	S 2c
Chappell, R.P.	F Ic	Childers, L.R.	S Ic
Christian, P.	Stm2c	Church, C. W.	S Ic
Ciapetti, D. R.	F Ic	Cliggott, J. P.	S Ic
Cohen, P.	Y2c	Colwell, I R.	EM3c
Conway, I S.	S Ic	Cook, Arthur E.	S 2c
Cook, Glen M.	S 2c	Cook, Harold H.	S 2c
Cook, Horace H.	S 2c	Crane, Frank I	Ylc
Crick, A. B.	S 2c	Cunningham, R. C.	S 2c
Currier, P.M.	F Ic	Dahle, I E.	S 2c
Davies, R. L.	S 2c	Davis, I E.	Stmlc
Day, R. L.	S Ic	Dennis, 1. E.	S 2c
Dennison, R. F.	S Ic	Dilliplane, A. F.	S 2c
Dowd, I I	EMIc	Dresnek, H.G.	EM 2c
Dumala, I A.	WT 3c	Durham, S. D.	F 2c
Elliott, I R.	SoM3c	Ellis, IT.	S 2c
Emerson, R. E.	S 2c	Enfield, I D.	CM 3c
Engel, D. F.	S Ic	Fick, E. 1.	S 2c
Fields, D.	S 2c	Fields, W.	S 2c
Foley, G. D.	SKD2c	Francis, H.J.	S Ic
Gallagher, G. E.	EM3c	Gallant, T. R.	BM2c
Garland, G.L.	S Ic	Garner, K. M.	S Ic
Garthwaite, S.J.	S 2c	Gary, G. W.	Stm2c
Gazda, H. I	S 2c	Golden, S. G.	S 2c
Goldfarb, A- I	FC3c	Goodnow, F. R.	S Ic
Gordon, I B.	S Ic	Grak, L. F.	RMIc
Gray, T. B.	S Ic	Green, R. L.	S Ic
Greer, W. H.	F 2c	Gunheim, G. G.	SoM3c
Guy, C.	S 2c	Hancock, D. G.	S 2c
Harder, R.	SM Ic	Harrill, E. R.	S 2c
Heaton, U. H. P.	F 2c	Henrich, G. C.	GM3c
Henry, C. I	F 2c	Henry, Sherman	S 2c
Hensley, H. L.	S 2c	Herbert, C. J.	MM3c
Hetrick, M. M.	S 2c	Hinz, H. T.	PhM3c
Hogan, A. L.	MoMM2c	Hogan, M. I	MM3c
Holcum, W. D.	MM1c	Holie, 0.	CM1c
Hospidor, M. A.	SF 2c	Houghtaling, E. R.	SC1c
Hurteau, R. C.	F 2c	Innocenzi, I P.	S 2c
Jackson, E. D.	CMM	Jones, W. C.	S 2c
Jones, W. W.	F 2c	Keegan, R.J.	MM1c
Killaby, LA	S 2c	Kiser, E. L.	F 1c
Knight, E. H.	MM2c	Kollhoff, D. L.	F 2c.
Korel, B.	S 2c	Kreiser, C.E.	F 2c
Krepkin, H.	S 1c	Krouch, R. G.	RM1c
Krupa, E. J.	F 2c	Kyber, R. J.	Y3c

LaFargue, J. W.	S 2c	Lafferty, H. L.	EM2c
Laurie, A.	S lC	Lea, G. W.	S 1c
Lee, M. E.	SM 3c	Leigh, G.	F 1c
Lichniak, S.	F 1c	Little, C. K.	F 1c
Long, J. T.	S 2c	Loso, A. L.	S 2c
Lowrimore, F. S.	F 2c	Lutz, A- W.	QM1c
Martin, J. R.	MoMM1c	Martin, R. H.	S 1c
Mathis, 1. E.	CWT	Matkin, J. G.	S 2c
Matulich, H. V.	EM 2c	McClarg, H. E.	F 2c
Meckulch, T. G.	S 2c	Milner, R. E.	MM1c
Money, C. V.	RT3c	Moore, E. F.	WT3c
Morgan, J.J.	F 1c	Morin, J. L.	BKR1c
Mullett, N. H.	MM2c	Nagy, S. A.	S 2c
Navarro, R	S 1c	Nicolai, C.M.	WT3c
Nissen, A. F.	S 1c	Oellig, R. H.	S 1c
Osmialowski, V.J.	S 2c	Pagano, E,	F 1c
Pakiela, S. G.	SC1c	Paquin, F. T.	S 2c
Paul, Jack D.	F 1c	Perkins, R. A.	BM2c
Pettitt, R. A.	S 1c	Porter, W. A.	GM3c
Price, R.C.	GMIc	Prickers, W. B.	Stm2c
Purcell, E.K.	S 2c	Reese, J.M.	GM2c
Rice, E.	S 1c	Roberts, A.W.	S 1c
Robertson, E.	S 2c	Rodkey, C. L.	SC2c
Rupp, L. J.	EM2c	Schillaci, J. R.	F 2c
Schrad, H.H.	MM3c	Schuster, C.C.	F 2c
Scire, C. L.	RM2c	Scott, F. L.	RT2c
Scott, R. W.	GM3c	Seiple, J. W.	QM3c
Shaffer, R. W.	WT2c	Shay, L. F.	MM2c
Skelton, G. R.	SoM1c	Slaven, A. E.	S 2c
Slesinski,' F.	WT2c	Smith, W. J.	S 1c
Snorbus, J. R.	SC2c	Somerville, T. W.	F 1c
Sorel, JK. R.	S 1c	Spence, J. T. I SSM)	S 2c
Sutton, C. L	S 1c	Theisen, WR.	RdM2c
Towne, W. H.	SKIc	Urban, J. E.	S 2c
VanWilpe, W.E. [GM]	S 1c	Vaughn, L. E.	S 1c
Via, R. C.	S 1c	Wagner, J.J.	RM3c
Walker, R. L.	EM2c	Warner, H. C.	F le
Watson, R. A-	F 2c	Weeks, A- C.	S 1c
Weisenberger, C.L.	F 2c	West, L. W.	MM2c
White, N.E.	S 2c	Whitesides, C. L.	BT3c
Wiggins, H. W.	S 2c	Williams, R. L.	S 2c
Willis, D. B.	S 2c	Winkle, D.F.	F 1c
Wise, E. T. R.	S 2c	Phillips, J.C.	SN

Bibliography

The oral histories as personally given are listed in this book. My own personal recollections and written notes on my Bassett experiences, plus conversations with Bassett shipmates, officers and family members of the crew are recalled.

Naval Archives, Washington D.C.
Ships logs on the dates of the sinking.
USS Indianapolis USS Bassett
USS Madison
other related material available at the Archives

The Explorer World Atlas--Rand McNally

World Book Encylopedia
Islands of the Pacific Ocean
****
Additional information is available from:

American Naval History
by: Jack Sweetman

The Two Ocean War
by: Samuel E. Morison

USS Indianapolis CA 35
by: Philip A. St. John, PhD

Abandon Ship
by: Richard Newcomb

Fatal Voyage
by: Dan Kurzman

REPRODUCED AT ...
U.S.A. LOG—LIST OF OFFICERS

LIST OF OFFICERS ATTACHED TO AND ON BOARD THE U.S.S. BARRETT (APB 57) COMMANDED

...R. THERIAULT, EDR, USNR., DURING THE PERIOD COVERED BY THIS LOG BOOK, WITH DATE OF

REPORTING FOR DUTY, DETACHMENT, OR DEATH, FROM   1 July   45   to   31 July   45

NAME AND FILE NUMBER	RANK	DATE OF REPORT OR DETACHMENT	PRIMARY DUTIES	NAME, RELATIONSHIP, AND ADDRESS OF NEXT OF KIN
R. THERIAULT 90480	Lt. Cdr.	23 Feb 45	Commanding	Mrs. H.J. Theriault – Wife, 3127 Riverside Ave., Jacksonville, Florida
J. W. HENDERSON 275484	Lieut.	23 Feb 45	Nav. Off.	Elizabeth W. Henderson, Wife, 202 Washington St., Middletown, Conn.
A. R. AXTELL 183352	Lieut.	27 Mar 45	First Lieut.	Lois Evelyn Axtell, Wife, 2765 Rivetwood Lane, Jacksonville (7), Florida
E. T. EVANS, Jr.	Lieut.	23 Feb 45	Gunnery Officer	Nadine G. Evans, Wife, 2209 West Avenue, Burlington, Iowa
M. W. FRUST 375278	Lt. (jg)	23 Feb 45	Medical Offr.	Mrs. Royce W. Frust, Wife, c/o Mr. E. A. Deckow, Eastland, Texas
W. T. ANDERSON 323020	Lt. (jg)	23 Feb 45	Engr. Offr.	Mrs. Celestor Mae Anderson, wife, 705 E. Chest St., Pensacola, Florida
G. K. VAN DYKE 348199	Ensign	23 Feb 45	Comm. Offr.	Jessie M. Van Dyke, 1820 Lakeshore avenue, Oakland, Calif.– Wife
E. E. HORWITZ 265089	Lt. (jg)	23 Feb 45	ASW Officer	Lt. A.K. Horwitz, brother, Brooks Convalescent Hosp. Annex 1, Ft. Sam Houston, Texas
O. W. LINDSEY 373451	Ensign	23 Feb 45	Supply Offr.	Margaret W. Lindsey, wife, 1121 Third Avenue, Laurel, Mississippi
J. LEWLEE 403361	Lt. (jg)	23 Feb 45	Asst. Engr. Officer	Mrs. Sam P. Lewlee, wife, 2233 Drury, Kansas City, 1, Missouri
A. DE LISLE 408323	Ensign	23 Feb 45	Asst. Comm. Officer	Mrs. James Ketchum, mother, 3737 E. 104th St., Cleveland, 11, Ohio
L. F. WORK 333549	Ensign	18 Apr 45	Asst. First Lieutenant	Lt. (jg) W. Work, USCGR, brother, 3011 Noble Ave., Richmond, 22, Virginia
HAGER 413066	Ensign	29 May 45	Asst. Boat Officer	Mrs. Warren L. Hager, mother, 501 Woods Ave., Flemington, Pa.
J. BROSER 409606	Ensign	23 Feb 45	Boat Offr.	Mrs. Navy Broser, mother, 1695 Selwyn Avenue, Bronx, New York
SNOOK 442300	Ensign	28 July 45	Asst Gunnery Officer	Mrs. J. M. Snook, mother, 3612 Lakeshore Oakland, (10) Calif.

J. W. HENDERSON, Lieut.   U.S.N.R., NAVIGATOR.

189

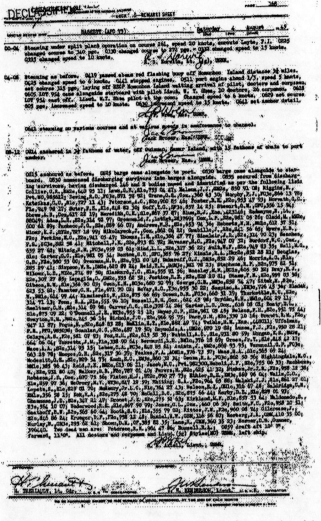

An enlarged copy of this log was inserted with purchase of book.

190

Remember the Indy

This is the story of men you should know
  Who sailed on a great ship fifty years ago*
They crossed the Pacific on a mission of great destiny
  To bring a powerful force to the Philippine sea.

Their mission was completed and the historic errand run
  But their struggle for life had just begun.
The ship was sunk in a midnight watery grave
  Taking a large part of the crew, so young and so brave.

Survivors few drifted on an oil blackened sea
  And rescuers were slow in answering their plea.
Five days they drifted with salt, sun and shark
  Adding more graves but leaving no mark.

The few that survived now tell the tale
  Of how the ship succeeded on this historic sail.
The bomb was delivered and the world would soon know
  What man had created on this earth below.

Japanese cities gave evidence of an atomic race
  And now this power takes its worldly place.
We honor the living and mourn the loss of our men
  And we pray that this power will never be used again.

We "Remember Pearl Harbor" and the "USS Maine"
  Let's add a new motto to this old refrain.
"Remember the Indy" and the crew she gave;
  And by the bomb millions of lives were saved!

L. Peter Wren
Rescue Officer•USS Bassett [APD 73]
*The USS Indianapolis [CA35] was sunk 30 July 1945

191

Definitions of Navy Abbreviations

ANFSWP - Allied Naval Forces Southwest Pacific also known as "MacArthur's Navy"

APD - Attack/Personnel/Destroyer e.g. Fast Troop Transport

CINC PAC - Commander in Chief – Pacific Fleet

Comphiblant - Commander-Amphibrous Forces-Atlantic Fleet

CNO - Chief of Naval Operations

CO - Commanding Officer

HECP - Harbor Entrance Control Post

LCT - Landing Craft-Carrying Tanks and Personnel

LCVP - Landing Craft-Vehicles/Personnel

P.I. - Philippine Islands

PSF - Philippine Sea Frontier

SOPA - Senior Officer Present Afloat/Ashore

T.H. - Territory of Hawaii

5th/7th Fleet - Different commands in charge in different Pacific Ocean areas

ORDER FORM

If you would like additional copies of this book, in
either softcover or hardcover, please contact

L. Peter Wren LCDR USNR Ret.
1011 Ridge Top Road
Richmond, VA 23229

The price for the softcover version is $11.95, and the
price for the hardcover version is $21.95.